Get the Edge at Roulette

A Scoblete Get-the-Edge Guide

Get the Edge at Roulette

How to Predict Where the Ball Will Land!

by Christopher Pawlicki

Foreword by Frank Scoblete

Bonus Books, Inc.
Chicago, Illinois

04 03 02 01 00   5 4 3 2 1

Library of Congress Card Number: 2001090191
ISBN: 1-56625-160-5

Bonus Books, Inc.
160 East Illinois Street
Chicago, Illinois 60611

Printed in the United States of America

To my beautiful and devoted wife, Deanna, whose support made the completion of this book possible. And to my three bright and energetic children, Brian, Brent and Brooke, who help me to mainain that child-like curiosity that motivated me to research and undertake this project.

Table of Contents

Foreword

In the past, many mathematically oriented gaming writers would look at a game such as roulette, figure out its mathematical underpinnings, recognize that the game could not be beaten, warn their readers to watch their money and then these writers would turn their attention to other, more hopeful games, such as blackjack and poker.

In the past, many gamblers would look at a game such as roulette and think to themselves that there has to be a way to beat it. These same gamblers invented all sorts of systems, most of which were mathematical, to beat roulette—and every single one of them failed in the long run. Many went broke as they had also put their money where their faulty math was.

If roulette is its math then the game is unbeatable. After all, the casino takes a hefty slice of every winning bet—on straight-up bets in Europe, on the single-zero wheel, they pay a winner 35 to 1 instead of 36 to 1, and in America, on the double-zero wheel, they pay the winner that same 35 to 1 instead of 37 to 1. In both Europe and America they pay even-money on bets that are 19 to 18 and 10 to 9 favorites, respectively, for the house. The list goes on but you get the picture. You can't win in the long run when you're bucking the kinds of house edges you find at roulette (single-zero = 2.70 percent and double-zero = 5.26 percent).

However, as is usual with games that have a physical component, the choice is not between the mathematicians' despair and the gamblers' fallacies, because there is a third option in designing methods to beat these games. *Attack their physicality.* In craps, for example, that translates into attempting to control your rolls to avoid the 7 and/or hit specific numbers more than probability would dictate, and designing betting strategies to exploit those shooters who just might have these abilities. In roulette, the physical nature of the game—the spinning wheel and the dealer who starts the ball rolling (so to speak)—can also be attacked.

Enter Christopher Pawlicki, whose nickname, the Spindoctor, is the proper appellation for this brilliant young man who has worked out and/or perfected just about every conceivable legal method for beating roulette. Enter this book, the third of my *Scoblete Get-the-Edge Guides*, where the Spindoctor is going to make a house call directly to you. Once you've read this book, you will know exactly what has ailed the body of your roulette play in the past and exactly what the prescription is to remedy it.

In my opinion *Get the Edge at Roulette: How to Predict Where the Ball Will Land* is the greatest roulette book ever written for the player who is serious about just that—getting an edge by predicting where the ball will land! It is not the easiest book to comprehend because some of the methods of attacking the physical nature of roulette require fierce concentration and an understanding of the math behind the technique. But if you stick with the Spindoctor's analysis and advice, you will discover ways to literally get an edge at roulette.

Here are just some of the wonderful things the Spindoctor has for you in this book:

He shows how to find and play *biased wheels*; how to recognize and exploit *deep-pocket wheels* that are more susceptible to bias tracking. He shows you *visual wheel tracking* techniques that can give you the edge by *visually predicting* where the ball is most likely to land. In addition, he will show you how to sector slice to increase the speed and accuracy of your predictions.

For the first time ever, Pawlicki describes the method he uses for detecting *dealer signatures* and *relative numbers*, a devastating approach to roulette that plays the dealer as well as the wheel. He also shares with you his experiences as a dealer who can hit his number on a more than random basis.

Finally, Pawlicki discusses the new world of Internet roulette and how it differs from the real-world game—and what you can do to maximize your ability to bring home the money from cyberspace. In fact, he shows you two ways that guarantee that you can beat Internet casinos!

Utilizing his expertise in physics, mathematics and computer science, Christopher Pawlicki has applied his awesome knowledge towards discovering and developing the best physical methods of beating roulette. If you want the best chance to win at the wheel, this is the book for you!

Part 1

The Background Spin

A Brief History of the Game

Have you ever found yourself being mesmerized by the spinning little white ball orbiting the outer wheel like some celestial satellite, then, spiraling down to meet a whirl of blacks, reds and greens, taking a few bounces and then a final rendezvous with fate? The game of roulette has fascinated casino patrons for close to 300 years now. Although no one seems to know all of the details surrounding its origin and development, some form of the game is probably as old as the wheel itself.

There are accounts of ancient Romans tipping their chariots on their sides and spinning one of the wheels for games of amusement. The word roulette is French, meaning "little wheel." Several early versions of roulette appeared in Europe during the 17th and 18th centuries. It is believed that the noted French scientist and mathematician Blaise Pascal invented the mechanism in 1657 while experimenting with perpetual motion devices. It is thought that he named his device roulette, however he did not envision its use for gambling. Pascal, incidentally, pioneered the mathematical field of probability.

One early account that we have of a spinning ball and rotating horizontal wheel being used as a gaming device was in a game called roly-poly in 1720. Here, the ball was spun inside the outer edge of the bowl and the rotor was propelled in the opposite direction, just like the game we know today. When the ball sufficiently slowed in the upper track, the gravitational force overcame the centripetal force and the ball was pulled down towards the spinning rotor. It eventually came to rest in one of its many pockets.

The Gaming Acts of 1739 and 1740 banned roly-poly, as well as many other games of chance in England. An innovative Beau Nash, the Master of Ceremonies at Bath, England, evaded these laws by introducing EO, or even-odd, but that too was outlawed in 1745. During the next 50 years, the game evolved into the one we recognize today.

The modern wheels appeared in Paris casinos around 1796. They contained all of the familiar elements that survive today, the alternating red and black colors, the layout of numbered pockets 1 through 36, the 0 and the 00. About the only difference being that the single zero was red in color (although the casino barred any red bets from winning if 0 appeared) and the double zero was black (again barring black bets). To alleviate the confusion, the color green was eventually assigned to the zeros.

This version of roulette found its way over to the U.S. by way of Europeans in New Orleans in the early 1800s. Some proprietors, not content with a big 5.26 percent edge, experimented with wheels containing 31 pockets. These wheels were numbered 1 through 28, with a 0, 00 and an Eagle pocket. These greedy proprietors paid out only 26 to 1 for a single number win (30 to 1 is the fair pay out). This translates into a whooping 12.9 percent house edge! People soon stopped playing these wheels in favor of the original double-zero wheels.

Meanwhile back on the continent, two innovative brothers from France went in the opposite direction. Francois and Louis Blanc introduced the first single-zero roulette wheel in 1842. They left France, where gambling was illegal, and set up a house in Homburg, Bavaria (now Germany). The new single-zero wheel, with a 2.7 percent edge instead of the double zero's 5.26 percent edge, was an instant hit. It decimated the competition. When gambling was outlawed in Germany, Louis Blanc (who survived his brother) accepted an invitation from the Prince of Monaco, Charles III, for whom Monte Carlo was named. For a cost of two million francs, he was allowed to establish and operate the magnificent casino that still sets all the standards in Europe.

Although both the double- and single-zero wheels originated in France, the double zero became known as the American wheel, because it survived in the States. The popularity of the single-zero wheel had supplanted the double-zero wheel in Europe and consequently was dubbed the French wheel. In Europe, the option of *en prison* was offered, further lowering the house edge on even money wagers down to 1.35 percent! No wonder the game accounts for over 50 percent of revenues in European casinos as compared to about 5 percent in U.S. casinos. Casinos in Atlantic City offer a version of *en prison* called surrender for even-money bets on their double-zero wheels. This effectively reduces the casino's edge from 5.26 percent to 2.63 percent for those bets.

Roulette did enjoy popularity stateside around the turn of the century until World War II. As Americans learned to lose less at craps and subsequently became interested in the notion that blackjack was beatable, roulette declined in popularity. Roulette is the oldest casino game still in existence. I believe that with the emergence of more single-zero wheels in the United States and a well-informed gambling public, the game may enjoy a resurgence in popularity.

Why We Play Roulette

Anticipation

Betting, waiting, watching. The ball makes its passes in the outer rim, gradually slowing down and breaking from the upper track. Spiraling down to the rotor, the ball crosses over, strikes a numbered pocket, then a few short hops later, hopefully comes to rest in one of our favorite numbers. It's easy to get caught up in the excitement as the event unfolds right before your eyes. I can't imagine feeling more excited than seeing the ball enter the rotor right before my targeted sector of pockets and watching as it dribbles right into one of my heavily favored numbers. What an adrenaline rush! Or the ball descends half a wheel away, but through the benefit of a strange bounce, it is suspended on the rotor's edge . . . waiting for my area to come into play! Then, bam, it takes a turn right into one of my pockets.

Of course, the reverse happens as well. Either way, it is a roller coaster ride of emotions. It is the highs and the lows that make it thrilling. Will I experience the depression of a near miss? Or will I enjoy the nirvana of a straight up win? Hold onto your seats, folks!

Tradition

What's a casino without a roulette wheel? Imagine Rick's Café in the movie *Casablanca* or James Bond's savvy wagering without a roulette wheel around. In fact, countless movies with scenes situated in a casino will frequently show a roulette wheel to help the viewer realize, "Yeah, we're in a casino now." Without question, the roulette wheel has been the dominant symbol of casino gambling. From movies to television shows to photographs, a roulette wheel is usually front and center in the camera's attention . . . and why not?

Roulette is the oldest of all the modern casino games, dating back almost 300 years. Couple this long history with romantic notions of breaking the bank, and you have an irresistible lure. There are plenty of stories to go around of big wins and near misses. Ask anyone of the patrons playing roulette. They'll usually have some personal stories to share. Perhaps they even know some of the romantic tales of past heroes who tempted fate and were victorious.

My favorite roulette story starts off: "One of the most spectacular and popular gamblers at Monte Carlo was a handsome young American named William Nelson Darnborough from Bloomington, Illinois. How he beat roulette at Monte Carlo from 1904 to 1911 has been a well-kept secret." Darnborough, in fact, beat the casino to the extent of $415,000. That's a sum, no doubt, equal to 10 or 15 times that amount in today's dollars. If you would like to read the rest of the story, it's in **Part 4.**

Diversification

There's something for everyone in roulette, from the more conservative even-money bettor to the more aggressive long-shot artist, and every kind of bettor in between. There's a bet to go with every temperament. Unlike the game of craps with its diversity of wagers, the house's edge at roulette is consistent for all wagers, from conservative betting all the way up to the 35-to-1 straight up wagers. The French 2.7 percent edge or even the American 5.26 percent edge is far better than the double-digit edge found on the center of a craps table.

Because of the variety of wagers, many systems have been developed over the past couple of hundred years with roulette in mind. Whether it's the Martingale, the Labouchere, the d'Alembert or a half-dozen others that come to mind, there are numerous betting systems available to employ. And now, with the popularity of the electronic tote board, systems players can easily canvas a given wheel for various combinations of results before wagering. Of course there is no way to beat the game with a purely mathematical approach, but when applied in moderation, certain betting systems will help enhance your enjoyment of the game as well as your accounting skills.

Appreciation

Some folks just develop an appreciation for the finer things in life. Adding a touch of sophistication makes life interesting. Things like art, music, fashion or fine dining help us to develop a more civil side to our personality. As an engineer, I appreciate the precision crafted mechanism of a casino roulette wheel on one hand, along with the richly appointed hardwoods and chrome trim on the other. Like a fine Swiss watch or an expensive German auto, today's roulette wheels are a beautiful mixture of old-world craftsmanship and state-of-the-art manufacturing technology. Just like the automobile or the watch, a finely tuned roulette wheel is a joy to observe.

Recreation

The game can be an elegant, leisurely break from the rest of the casino. With a sense of civility and decorum, where else can the common folk and the aristocracy both share the plush surroundings of a relaxed and quiet atmosphere? Roulette is often characterized as a serious, but unhurried game, graced by Kings and Queens. With plenty of time between spins, you'll have ample opportunity to play your systems. You can calculate your next series of wagers or socialize with neighbors. Relax and enjoy the company of that attractive blond on your right or that shapely brunette on your left who needs assistance reaching the layout. Of course, not wanting to appear sexist in any way, how about rubbing elbows with that dashing young Duke, or some friendly conversation with that handsome, witty Texan?

You can make an event out of playing roulette. Because of its slower, more relaxed pace, you can stop and enjoy the company at hand. Indeed, the game is faster here in the States, but you can still stop to chat with your neighbors if you're feeling social. In North America, only a small percentage of gamblers consider roulette to be their favorite game, but it can provide a welcome diversion for players who want to relax before getting back to the more fast-paced casino games such as craps and blackjack.

Remuneration

Naturally, the biggest reason that many people play roulette is to make money! Whether playing systems or hunches, everyone seems to have an opinion on the proper method of play. If we thought that we had no chance of winning, we simply would not play. Most patrons will play if they feel they have some chance to beat the game, even if it's a win based on pure luck—as it is when you employ most betting schemes at roulette.

But is it possible to beat this game over the long term? Is it possible to get the edge at roulette? I believe it is . . . if (and that's a big IF) you have the proper strategy and the dedication to know how to employ it. While mathematical systems alone will fail in the long run, the right predictive methods can and have beaten the game. In later sections of this book we'll discuss such topics as dealer's signature, biased-wheel play and visual tracking, to name a few. These are the kinds of techniques that dedicated players can employ to get the edge because they predict where the ball is going to land, albeit these predictions are probabilistic and not perfect.

Table Etiquette on Both Sides of the Atlantic

Different Worlds

In Europe, roulette is an immensely popular game. It is a comfortable, quiet, leisurely game usually enjoyed by the fairer sex and systems players (those players using a betting, but not a predictive system to try to overcome the house edge). The table limits are higher and the house edge is smaller. When you consider the fact that there is only one zero (37 pockets instead of 38), the house edge is brought down to 2.7 percent. Then add to that the *en prison* rule for even-money wagers and you'll find the edge cut down to a less formidable 1.35 percent—which makes these bets better than the pass and come bets at craps, Let It Ride, Three Card Poker, Caribbean Stud, Pai Gow Poker and a host of other games and wagers!

If you think you might visit any of the European casinos, plan ahead. Find out if they have a dress code. The more elegant casinos will require formal dress. Also, the casinos may actually be private clubs, open only to club members and their guests. This is especially true in the United Kingdom. After you apply for membership, you will have to wait at least 24 hours before playing. Be wary and learn the proper manners, for example in many European casinos tipping the dealer may not be allowed. Before visiting these establishments for the first time, remember to do your homework.

The casinos in the United States and Canada have a much different atmosphere. North American games run two to three times faster. You'll probably find a more casual dress code and a laid-back attitude. On one recent visit to Las Vegas, I watched as two young couples, sprinkling the layout and swiggin' beer, were having an amusing and uninhibited time at one of the roulette tables at the California Club.

Whenever one of them would hit a straight-up winner, all four would jump to their feet, banging backsides and singing "Roller coaster . . . of love." I have to admit, everyone was enjoying themselves, including the dealer and the supervisor. But what a contrast to the more reserved and slower paced games found on the continent. You won't find many people slapping their backsides but you will still find that roulette is a roller coaster!

Of course, the standards are different in America and Canada as well. For example, in American casinos tipping the dealer is not only permitted, it is encouraged, and dealers rely on tips to make a living. Unfortunately, on average, the North American roulette game is not as good as its European cousin. It is possible to find single-zero wheels in Las Vegas and you can find the surrender rule (similar to the *en prison* rule) in Atlantic City, but I have not seen both available at the same casino, or even in the same city.

En Prison vs. Surrender

Now is probably a good time to explain the difference between the European *en prison* rule and the Atlantic City surrender rule. In Europe, when the single-zero comes up, all even-money wagers—red/black, odd/even, high/low—are frozen (or put *en prison*) until a nonzero number results, deciding the bet's fate. If the bet wins on the subsequent spin, then it is returned to the bettor (a push). If it is not a winner, then it is lost.

Here's an example: You wager $5 on red. If red comes up immediately, you win $5, getting back $10 total. If black comes up, you lose, but if green (0) comes up, you wouldn't necessarily lose. You have a chance to get your original bet back. If red appears on the next spin, then you would receive your $5 back, with no winnings. If black is the result, you lose. You would remain in prison if green appears again. This effectively cuts the house edge in half, from 2.7 percent down to 1.35 percent for all even-money wagers.

Surrender also cuts the house edge in half for even-money wagers, but it works a little differently. If you had put that same $5 bet on red in Atlantic City, and a zero or double zero (green) appeared, then the dealer would immediately give you half your wager back ($2.50). The Atlantic City casinos don't wait for the next spin to decide if you get $0 or $5 back. They split the difference and settle right away. Thus the casino's edge is cut from 5.26 percent down to 2.63 percent for even-money bets.

Table Layout and Seating

In Europe, you'll usually find two betting layouts with one single-zero wheel in between. The spinner, or croupier operates the wheel. Two dealers on either side watch the betting layout and assist with placing bets. In Europe, dealers often place about 80 percent of the wagers. Aside from the extra dealers, there is usually an inspector or boss who presides over the game. Interestingly, the Inspector must have the ability to recall all of the bets that were placed and whom they belong to, for the previous two spins! This is done to help alleviate confusion. One wheel can accommodate 12 to 16 seated players.

In North America, one wheel per betting layout is customary. The wheel is positioned at the far end beyond the top of the betting layout. Most times one dealer is stationed behind the wheel and controls the entire game. A floating supervisor or boss will monitor two tables at a time. These games will accommodate five or six seated patrons, but sometimes a second row of players will stand behind them. I've seen 10 to 12 patrons squeezing in to play at one table. In North America, the dealers assist with placing only about 20 percent of the wagers. Usually a second dealer will help to sort out chips when the action gets hot.

If you wish to sit and relax, find an open seat. If you have the option, select a seat that fits your needs. For example if you are a wheel watcher, you'll probably appreciate sitting right next to the wheel. I call this first base. From this position you can easily see the wheel and cover the top and middle of the betting layout. The next position, I call center field, is the best seat for reaching the entire betting baize. With great access to the layout and good visibility of the wheel, this is probably my favorite seat. The third position (last seat on the straightaway) is second base. This seat offers the worst view of the wheel. You will need assistance from the dealer if you wish to place wagers at the top of the layout. Just around the corner are two seats that directly face the wheel. Keeping with our baseball analogy, these would be shortstop and third base. Reaching for anything beyond the third dozens would require quite a stretch, but they are usually afforded a good view of the action. Sometimes a sixth chair is positioned around the corner from third base (same side of the table as the dealer). This player can access most of the layout and has a great view of the wheel as well.

The European tables may have one or two additional seats on the same side of the table that the dealer occupies. Another option, which I usually accept, is to stand. I like to watch the wheel from behind the seated first base player. After the seated players have placed most of their bets, and the dealer has commenced spinning the ball, I reach over between first and center and place my bets. Usually a quick "excuse me please" is all that is required for them to give you some room.

Wheel Chips vs. House Chips

In Europe, all players bet with the same house checks (or chips). Sometimes, if the game heats up, the confusion is very real. Imagine that you're down to your last few chips. You place one each on 26, 0 and 32. The ball crosses onto the

rotor near 7, strikes 35 and dribbles into 26! Just as you reach
for your winnings, another patron has firmly wrenched his
hands around your winning stacks, claiming them as his. But
you know that you wagered on the 0 and its two neighbors.
Everyone looks at you as though you were trying to pull a fast
one! Unfortunately, this scenario has probably happened
many times before. Just make sure to keep your guard up at
all times. Betting the same number of chips each spin will
help. If you are betting neighbors (forming a sector) or
favorite numbers, it will be easier to locate your bets. If you
are just sprinkling the layout as you see fit with no particular
pattern to speak of, then you may lose track of your wagers
too easily.

In North America, the roulette games use special chips
called wheel chips. These chips will have a unique letter or
design on them designating which table they belong to. They
cannot be used anywhere else in the casino, only at the table
from which they were issued. The wheel chips come in six or
seven different color groups of 300 chips each. Each seated
player will usually have his own color to bet with, eliminating any confusion on the layout.

After the dealer has paid off all the winning bets from
the previous spin, place your buy-in (cash or casino checks)
out on the layout and ask if there is a color available. You cannot hand the money to the dealer; place it down on the table.
If the dealer does not see your buy-in right away, be patient;
he may be busy. But do keep an eye on it until he is ready to
convert it. He will count out your money or chips on the table
in front of him. After getting a final check from the supervisor, he will push your colored wheel chips over to you.

You can buy in for any amount that you wish, as long
as it is equal to or greater than the minimum bet allowed on
that table (check the placard located near the wheel itself).
The wheel chips are organized into stacks of 20. If the chip
minimum for that table is 25 cents (downtown Vegas) and
you give the dealer a $5 bill, he will assume that you want

(20) 25-cent chips to play with. If, instead, you want (10) 50-cent chips or (5) $1 chips, you will have to inform him of your preference. There is a shelf on the back rim of the roulette wheel where one of each colored chip can be placed. The dealer will place a special marker button, or lammer on your color to signify what it is worth. You can make your wheel chips worth the minimum, usually 25 cents, 50 cents or $1, $5, $25 each or up to $100 each in certain casinos, depending upon the amount of your buy-in. If you wish to play with chips worth more than $100 in value, talk to one of the bosses in the pit to see if they can accommodate you. No other person can use your chips to bet with, not even your own spouse, who may be standing right behind you.

Chips are cleared and moved by hand in North American casinos instead of by rake. You will notice that winning wagers are paid by cutting the chips. Dealers will bring their entire hand over a stack of chips and use the index finger to cut and separate chips into smaller stacks. Outside bets are simply paid off in like stacks. The dealer doesn't actually count the chips. He will pay you in two same-height stacks for 2-to-1 wagers or one equal stack for even-money bets. Winning bets are paid in Europe by running out the chips. Because the French-style chips are beveled on-edge and more awkward to handle, the winning bet is spread out left to right in front of the dealer and counted out precisely. This of course, accounts for much of the extra time taken.

After the dealer has paid off all the winning bets, he will remove the marker, or dolly from the winning number and place it near the wheel. This is your signal to begin betting. Players are given time to decide where they want to put their chips on the layout. After most bets appear to be placed, the dealer will commence spinning the ball. In North America, the dealer will typically spin the wheel head counterclockwise (CCW) and snap the ball in the clockwise (CW) direction. In Europe, the croupier will alternate directions on subsequent spins. The ball is always spun in the opposite direction that the wheel is spun. You may continue to wager after the ball is snapped, but only until the dealer cries, "no more bets," and waves his arm over the layout. In French, the croupier would call out, *"rien ne va plus"* as he waves both arms out to the sides.

Recently, many European casinos have set up special rooms offering American games. They have adapted many of the American innovations like square-edge chips and a set of differently colored wheel chips for each table. Like the games in North America, these games clip along at a faster pace. As the inefficiencies of the French-style games become more apparent, I believe that the slower French games will give way to the faster and more profitable (to the casino) American style of play.

You must bet the table minimum on each spin (or nothing at all). If the table minimum is $5 and the chip minimums are $1 each, then each outside bet that you place must equal $5. The outside bets include the even-money wagers and the 2-to-1 wagers found on the outside of the layout. Any bets on an individual number (placed on the inside of the layout) are referred to as inside bets. These only need to total up to the table minimum. So, for our $5 table, you could place one $1 chip on the 1–4 line, one on the number 5 straight up, one on the 16-19 split, one on the 10-street and one chip on the 17-21 corner to fulfill the minimum requirement for inside betting. At the same time if you wish to wager on red and the second dozens, for instance, you will have to put down a complete and separate $5 bet on each one. Any additional outside bets will have to be $5 each.

Once the ball settles into one of the numbered pockets, the dealer will mark the winning number. All losing bets are immediately removed from the layout. Winning bets are paid according to the proper odds offered by the casino. Before leaving the table, you must color-up your wheel chips at that table (where you received them). Stack them neatly into piles of 5, 10 or 20 chips each and announce to the dealer, "Color coming in." Push your stacks carefully over to the dealer. He will recount your chips, check their value, and pay you in regular casino chips.

If the table is not busy, or you only wish to place a few quick bets, then use the regular casino chips. Most dealers won't mind if nobody else is using them. Just check with the dealer first. Also, if you confine your betting to the outside bets, then the regular house chips are fine. Unlike the inside bets, keep your bet separate from anyone else's. Stack your bet with the larger denominations on the bottom and the smallest denomination on top. Organizing your wager in this way will make it easier for the dealer to make quicker and more accurate payoffs. Whether seated or standing at the table, conduct yourself with proper comportment. Sure, it's fine to enjoy yourself, but blowing smoke into people's faces, bumping or shoving the other patrons or using crude language is obnoxious, though sadly all too common behavior. A little respect for your fellow players will go a long way toward having a more pleasurable experience.

Various Wheel Wagers and Betting Baizes

The Ins and Outs of Betting

There are 38 different pockets that the ball can fall into (37 on the French-style wheel). Couple that with 11 different types of roulette wagers that you can make, and you have a host of ways to play your stake at the roulette table. You can go for the long shot or the more conservative even-money wagers. Either way, you're probably playing against the same house edge, unless you are taking advantage of the *en prison* or surrender options that may be available. We will look at each type of bet and three different types of layouts or betting baizes on which to make those bets. We'll cover each of the 11 wager types using the double-zero betting layout first, then we'll compare staking on the French single-zero layout. Six of these 11 types of bets are referred to as inside wagers and five are called outside wagers.

Inside wagers are made on the inside of the numbered betting grid. These are anything from a bet on a single number to a wager on a six-number group. They include a straight-up bet on one number, a split (two-number bet), a street (three-number wager), a corner which is a four-number stake, the top line (a five-number bet found only on the American layout) which covers the 00, 0, 1, 2 and 3 and finally the line, or six-number bet. As discussed in a previous section, all inside bets must at least add up to the table minimum, whereas each outside wager must be at least the table minimum.

The remaining five types of bets, or outside wagers, can be made along the outside of the numbered betting grid. The outside bets include the even-money and 2-to-1 wagers. These bets will have higher table maximums then the inside bets. Imagine a patron who likes the number 20 wagering $1,000 straight up on it. Each time that the number 20 comes up, he wins $35,000. The dealer falls into a pattern and hits three 20s in the next five spins . . . the casino would be down over $100,000 in a few minutes. Worse yet, if the dealer is skilled at sector shooting (the ability to have the ball land in a given sector of the wheel with more than random frequency) and has an accomplice betting a certain set of numbers for high stakes . . . well, you get the picture. A lot of money could change hands very quickly! The lower inside bet maximum prevents wild fluctuations (whether random or not) from killing the casino's potential profits. If, for example, the maximum bet on an inside number is $100, then the 2-to-1 wagers will probably permit a $1,000 bet and the even-money wagers will allow a $1,500 bet.

The even-money wagers are bets that cover groups of 18 numbers at a time. For example, there are 18 red numbers on the wheel. A bet on black or red, high or low, odd or even round out the three even-money wagers on the outside of the layout. Then we have a bet on any one of the dozens, be it the first, second or third, and a bet on one of the columns, again first, second or third. A dozen, or column bet is a twelve-number wager. Each of the inside and outside bets will be shown on what is commonly called the American double-zero layout. This layout is prevalent throughout North America and the Caribbean. Because there is both a single zero and double zero on the wheel itself, there are 38 total numbers that can be wagered upon. Hence, the betting layout will have 38 boxed numbers. **Diagram 1-A** is an American or double-zero layout with examples of one to four-number wagers. **Diagram 1-B** is also a double-zero layout with sample line bets and outside wagers depicted.

Inside Wagers

Straight-up Bet (One Number)

A straight-up bet is simply a bet on a single number. Because there are 38 numbers on an American double-zero wheel, there are 38 ways to make this bet. On our sample layout in **Diagram 1-A**, you will note that Chip A on number 8 and Chip B on number 25 are straight-up wagers. Be careful when placing a straight-up wager to place it directly on the number. If it touches a bounding white line, it may be confused with a split or corner bet and will pay a lot less.

If other chips are wagered on that number, then place your chip directly on top of theirs. Chip A is a wager that wins only if the number 8 comes up on the next spin. Likewise, Chip B wins if 25 is the result on the following spin. If any other number comes up, all bets not on the winning number are losers and are collected by the dealer. If a straight-up bet

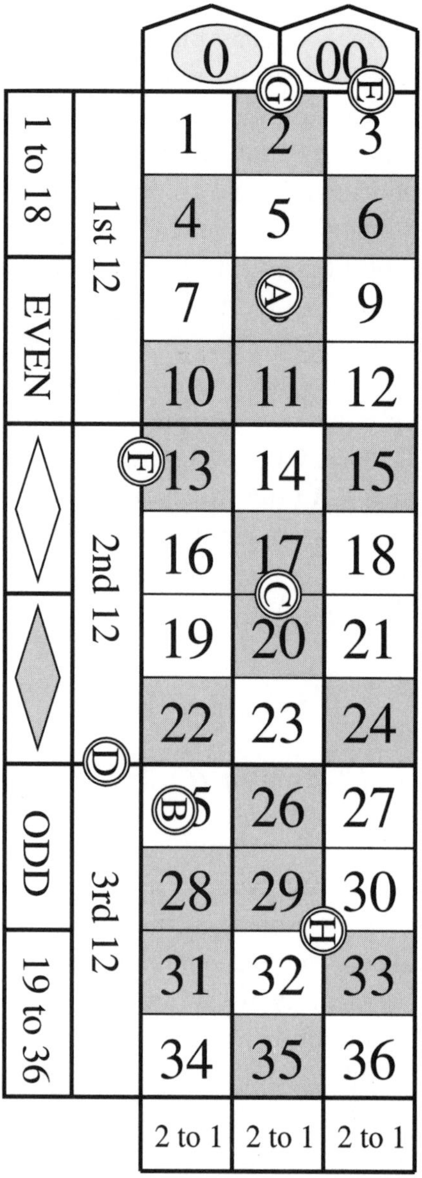

Diagram 1-A
American Double-Zero Layout

should win, then it will be paid at 35 to 1. If it were a fair game, you would be paid 37 to 1 for a double-zero wheel. By keeping the extra two chips for itself, the casino creates its 5.26 percent edge. Thus, for every one chip bet straight-up on the winning number, the player will receive 35 chips and the dealer will push two stacks (one of 20 and one of 15 chips) to you during the pay off. The original winning chip still belongs to you, but the dealer will leave it on the layout. You can, at your option, retrieve the chip after all of the payoffs are made or leave it there for the next spin.

I had one experience, a few years back at the Windsor Casino, where I wagered on the 12 and its four neighbors on the wheel (25, 29, 8 and 19). I was looking for one more hit to reach my win objective for the session and had placed five $5 chips out. The ball came down a little early around the 36 or 13, but I caught an extra bounce and held my breath as the ball came right into my area of the rotor. "Number 12, red and even," was the call! I was excited, winning 35 x $5 for a gain of $155 ($175 minus the four $5 bets I had on the neighbors). Two stacks of nickel ($5) chips were pushed over to me and I colored up the remaining $5 chips that I had stacked in front of me. In my excitement, I forgot to claim the original $5 chip before leaving the table. Another 12 was spun! I was half way over to the cashier's cage when an excited patron rushed up and pulled me back to the table to collect another $175! I was about to grab my original $5 stake from the layout after the second hit when the dealer and everyone else at the table admonished me to ride the hot number. I decided to have a little fun and instructed the dealer that the $5 bet was now for her and that if she could hit it a third time, she would collect the winnings. Her eyes got as big as saucers and she careful-ly built the wheel speed back up to its initial velocity and snapped the ball with that same patented release that attract-ed me to her table to begin with. By then, everyone had some-thing riding on the 12, but as luck would have it, the ball landed just two pockets shy in the 25. I threw her a $5 tip and headed back to the cashier's cage with an extra $170, all because I forgot to retrieve my original straight-up bet. I will discuss something called dealer's signature in **Part 5** and why you might consider intentionally leaving the chip out for the next spin.

Split Bet (Two Numbers)

A split bet is a wager on two different numbers that are next to each other on the betting layout. By centering a chip on a single line that separates two adjacent numbers, you can bet on both of those numbers with that one chip. Make sure that the chip does not touch a corner or it may be considered a four-number bet. There are 62 different ways to make a split bet. On our sample layout, **Diagram 1-A**, Chips C, D and E help illustrate how this bet can be made. Chip C is on the line between the 17 and 20, a popular split bet. If the 17 or 20 come in, the bet wins 17 to 1. Many casinos allow patrons at the far end of the table to split the zeroes by placing it on the courtesy line. Chip D is on the courtesy line, which separates the second and third dozens. If zero or double zero results, Chip D wins. Chip E is a split bet example on the 00 and 3. Because each chip has two numbers working for it, it pays 17 to 1. As always, your original chip will be left on the layout unless you take it or ask the dealer to take it down for you.

Street Bet (Three Numbers)

A street bet is a wager on three adjacent numbers that form a row on the betting layout. By placing a chip on the outside vertical line and aligning it with one of the first column numbers, you are betting on that particular number plus the two numbers on its right side forming a row. Chip F is situated on the 13 street. This is a three-numbered bet that covers 13, 14 and 15 with one chip. Placing three chips on the 13 street is effectively the same as playing the 13, 14 and 15 straight up for one chip each. The street bet pays 11 to 1 for each chip, so three chips will win you 33. When placing each number straight up with one chip, the two losing chips will be removed and the one winning chip will remain to pay 35 chips. Thirty-five chips minus two losing chips equals the same 33 chips net.

Make sure that the chip does not touch part of the number below (the 16 for our Chip F example) or above it (the 10). Otherwise, it will be considered a six-number bet instead of a three-number, or street bet. Chip G is placed right where the 0, 00 and 2 boxes all intersect. It is not a row, but it is a three-number bet covering those numbers. Also, the 0, 1 and 2 combination and the 00, 2 and 3 combination bets are made in a similar manner. Just place the chip where the three numbers intersect. If you look at the 12 different rows plus the three-number betting combinations involving zeroes, there are 15 different ways to make a street bet. If the 0, 00 or 2 came in on the next spin, then Chip G will win 11 to 1. Any other chips that do not have the winning number as part of their combination will be lost.

Corner Bet (Four Numbers)

A corner bet is a wager that covers four adjacent numbers. The bet is made by placing it at the intersection of the four numbers' box corners. On our double-zero layout, **Diagram 1-A**, Chip H is staked on the 29-33 corner. If any one of the numbers 29, 30, 32 or 33 comes in on the next spin, then Chip H will win. Be sure to center the chip over the point where all four numbers upon which you wish to wager intersect. There are 22 different ways that a corner bet could be made. Because the corner bet has four numbers working for it, it only pays 8 to 1. A $5 bet will pay $40. As described earlier, you can retrieve your original chip or leave it on the layout.

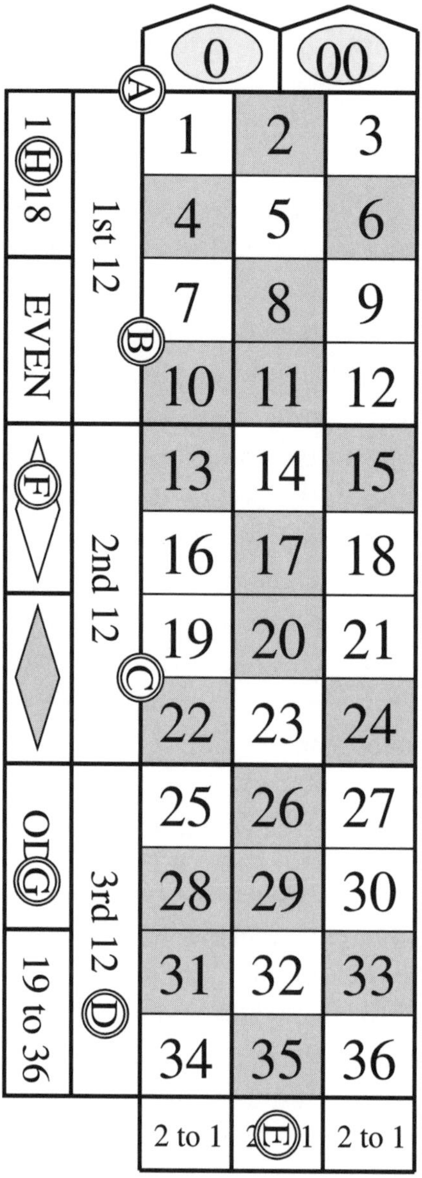

Diagram 1-B
American Double-Zero Layout

Top-line Bet (Five Numbers)

The top-line bet, which is the line that separates the zeroes from the 1, 2 and 3, is a five-number wager. It is the only way to make a five-number bet and it is only available on the American double-zero layout. By centering a chip where the 0, 1 and first 12 boxes intersect, you can bet on 0, 00, 1, 2 and 3 for the next spin. If the 0, 00, 1, 2 or 3 appear after the next spin, then the player wins six chips for every one wagered. There is only one way to make this bet. Chip A on **Diagram 1-B** illustrates how this bet is made on the double-zero layout. This is the only wager on the table that does not have the standard 5.26 percent house edge attached to it. Because there are 38 numbers on the layout, not 35 as the 6 to 1 payoff would indicate, this particular bet yields the house a huge 7.89 percent advantage. You are better off avoiding this bet altogether.

Line Bet (Six Numbers)

A line bet is a wager on a group, or block of six numbers. It is a stake covering two adjacent rows of three numbers each. Think of it as a double street bet. This wager pays 5 to 1. With one chip, you can wager on six sequential numbers starting with a first column number such as 1 (which covers 1 through 6) and going up to 31 (covering 31 through 36). By centering a chip over the intersection of two adjacent first-column numbers with one of the dozen's boxes, a line of six numbers can be wagered upon.

Chip B on **Diagram 1-B** illustrates how the numbers 7 through 12 can be wagered with just one chip. If Chip B represented two chips, then it would pay the same as placing one chip on the 7 street and the second on the 10 street. One chip bet on the correct street would pay 11 chips minus the one lost on the losing street for a net of 10 chips. Two chips staked on the correct line, paying 5 to 1, would also net 10 chips. Chip C is another example of the line bet, covering numbers 19 through 24. There are 11 different ways to make this six-number wager.

Outside Wagers

Dozen Bet (12 Numbers)

This bet takes numbers 1 through 36 and breaks them up into three groups of 12 numbers each. You can wager on numbers 1 through 12, 13 through 24, and 25 through 36, creating three different dozen bets. The top box that aligns with the left of the boxed numbers 1, 4, 7 and 10 covers numbers 1 through 12. It is labeled 1st 12. If any number from 1 through 12 comes in, then it will win two chips for every one wagered. The 2nd 12 box, found in the middle as you follow down the left side, lines up with numbers 13 through 24. These are the second-dozen numbers. Chip D in **Diagram 1-B** is wagered on the 3rd 12. This bet covers numbers 25 through 36 for the next spin. Place your wager separately from (not on top of) everyone else's. Be sure that it is totally inside the lines that bound that dozen box. The dozen bets are 12-number wagers paying 2 to 1.

Column Bet (12 Numbers)

The column bet is an outside wager that also covers twelve numbers. There are three different columns that you can wager on. At the bottom of the layout, you will spot three boxes with 2 to 1 printed in them. This is where you would place your chips if you intended to bet on the columns. Keep your bets separate from others and do your best to place them inside of the betting box. The 2-to-1 box under the 34 represents the first column. The 12 numbers directly above this box, starting with 1, 4, 7 . . . down to 28, 31 and 34 make up the first column group of numbers. Chip E in **Diagram 1-B** is a stake on the second-column numbers, 2, 5, 8 . . . down to 29,

32 and 35. The third-column numbers include the 3, 6, 9 . . . down to the 30, 33 and 36.

As with the dozen's bet, you can wager one chip in each of the first, second and third 12-number groups, hoping to stay even with the house (and enjoy "free" drinks and eats). I have seen some people actually try to do this. If any number from 1 through 36 came up on the next spin, the winning group would net two chips, but the two losing groups would each lose one, creating a break-even situation; this is the best scenario. Unfortunately, if the zero or double zero appears, then all three wagers will be lost . . . and if a string of zeroes ensues, you will be wiped out in short order.

Red or Black (18 Numbers)

On the outside of the layout in the center of the even-money wagers, you will see two boxes with diamonds in them. One diamond is solid red. Chip F is in this box (**Diagram 1-B**) and signifies a bet on any red number. If a red number does appear, then Chip F will win one chip, or even-money. Eighteen of the 38 numbers are red. The box containing the solid black diamond is where one would wager on any of the 18 black numbers. You will see many novice systems players running negative progressions on the red or black numbers. This is because they are the easiest to spot on the tote board and the easiest to reach on the betting layout. In **Part 2**, we will talk about mathematical systems and why they cannot win over a sustained period of play.

Odd or Even (18 Numbers)

Just to the left and right of the red and black wagers respectively, you will see a box marked "even" and a box marked "odd." An even wager is exactly that, a bet that an even number will result. There are 18 even numbers. The single and double zeroes are not even numbers. Chip G is a wager on the odd numbers. Every other number, starting with 1 and counting up to 35, is an odd number. Both of these bets pay 1 to 1.

Low or High (18 Numbers)

On the very top at the outside of the layout is a box marked "1 to 18." Technically, it should read "1 through 18" which are the numbers that this bet covers (it also pays 1 to 1). Chip H in **Diagram 1-B** is a bet on the low numbers. These include the numbers 1 through 18. At the outside bottom, is a betting box with "19 to 36" printed in it. Place your chip here if you wish to wager on the high numbers, 19 through 36, on the next spin. Low or high wagers pay even-money for a win.

The French Roulette Betting Layouts

You should now have a clear understanding of the various roulette wagers and how they are placed on the American double-zero betting layout. The American wheel and its layout refer to a wheel that has 38 different numbers. The French-style wheel only has 37 pockets (there is no 00). The payouts on the French wheel are the same for each bet type as the payouts on the American wheel (i.e. a straight-up bet pays 35 to 1). It is because of the extra pocket, while maintaining the same payout, that the American wheel's edge increases.

You may encounter two French layout styles in the casinos. The first is the style that you will see in North American casinos with single-zero wheels. This layout looks almost identical to the American double-zero layout except there is only one green zero found at the top of the layout. Everything is labeled in English and is easy to understand. Some American casinos will offer one single-zero wheel in the high rollers' area. Because there is no 00 present, and payoffs are still the same, the house edge is cut from 5.26 percent down to 2.7 percent. However, don't think that the American casinos are getting soft. What they lose in house edge, they make up for by imposing much higher table minimums on their single-zero wheels. As a result, they have half the edge but on at least twice and sometimes three or four times the minimum wager. Look at **Diagram 1-C** for an example of the French-style layout used in North America.

The second French-style layout is used in Europe and is a bit different. The inside numbered grid is very similar to the American style. Three columns of 36 numbers alternating red and black are printed on the layout. The single zero is up at the top. Because players in Europe are permitted to sit on both sides of the table and bet, the outside wagers flank both sides of the numbered grid. In addition, you will see French terminology used in the outside betting boxes to describe which group of numbers you are staking. **Diagram 1-D** illustrates the French-style layout used throughout Europe. We will take a quick look at each type of bet and its corresponding French terminology. In no time, you will be placing bets like James Bond in Monte Carlo!

En plein is identical to the straight-up wager found in North America. A player simply stakes his bet on the number of his choosing. It is a one-number (*un numero*) bet that pays 35 to 1 like its American counterpart. However, unlike its American cousin, you are shorted only one chip instead of two when paid. A French wheel with 37 different pockets should pay out 36 chips for each one wagered on a winning *en plein*. The correct odds for an American wheel with 38 pockets are 37 to 1. This shortage in payoff is what creates the casino's edge for this and other games it offers.

A *cheval* is a split bet on any two adjacent numbers. Just place your stake on the line that separates those two numbers. A *cheval*, or *deux numeros* bet pays 17 to 1 if either number wins. On the single-zero wheel, the correct pay out should be 17.5 to 1 for a fair game. On an American double-zero wheel, it should be 18 to 1.

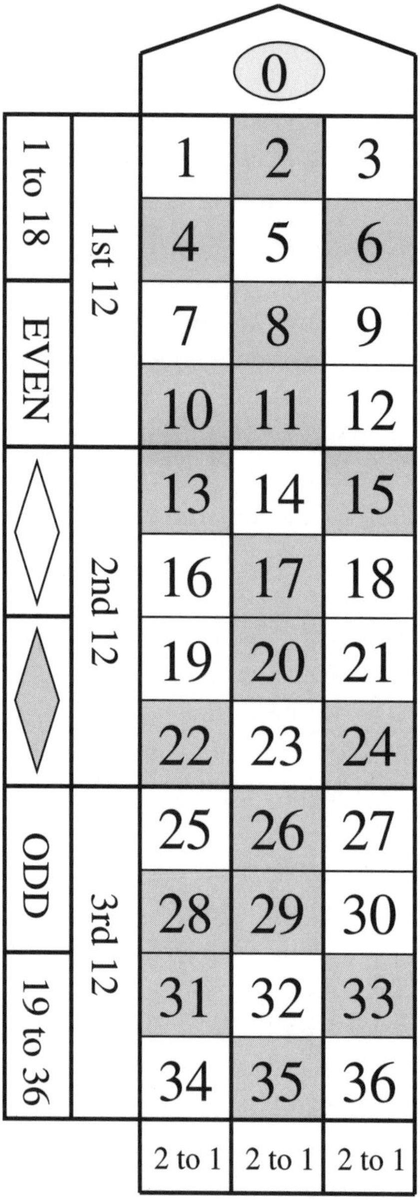

		0		
1 to 18	1st 12	1	2	3
		4	5	6
EVEN		7	8	9
		10	11	12
◇	2nd 12	13	14	15
		16	17	18
◆		19	20	21
		22	23	24
ODD	3rd 12	25	26	27
		28	29	30
19 to 36		31	32	33
		34	35	36
		2 to 1	2 to 1	2 to 1

Diagram 1-C
American Single-Zero Layout

Transversale pleine is a street bet covering any horizontal row of three numbers (*trois numeros*). By placing a chip on the outer vertical line in that chosen row, you will be wagering upon the three numbers contained in that row. As with the American layout, there are 12 such rows that can be wagered upon, but unlike the layout found stateside, there are only two three-number combinations possible with the single zero: 0, 1, 2 and 0, 2, 3.

En carre is a corner bet covering four numbers, or *quatre numeros*. By placing a chip where the four numbers' boxes all intersect, the player is wagering on the four numbers that the chip is touching. The one exception to this would be the top line wager, where the chip is placed on the outside vertical line and 1, 0 box intersection point, similar to the five-numbered wager on the American layout. Because there is no 00 present, the top line on the French layout becomes a four-numbered stake covering 0, 1, 2 and 3. The corner or top line wager pays 8 to 1.

The French-style layout contains no five-number, or *cinq-numeros wager*. I doubt if the Europeans miss it much. A five-number wager would pay 6 to 1. For every five chips that you bet on this imaginary line, you would win 30, being shorted 2 chips instead of 1. At –5.4 percent, this bet would carry twice the ordinary 2.7 percent edge the European casinos presently enjoy.

Sizain or *Six aine* (I've seen it both ways) refers to a line bet or *six numeros* wager. By placing a chip where the outer vertical bounding line and the line horizontally separating two streets intersect, a player can cover a block of six numbers. The line bet pays 5 to 1.

Colonne is the French term for column. Just as described previously regarding the American layout, small boxes located at the bottom of each column provide the necessary spaces to wager on one of these 12-numbered groups. Unlike their American cousin, the boxes are not marked with

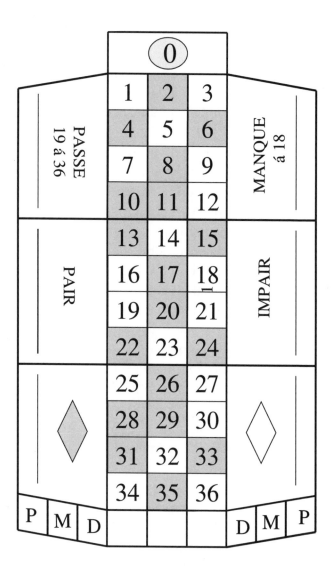

Diagram 1-D
European Single-Zero Layout

"2 to 1," however they do pay the same: two chips for every one wagered.

Douzaine is French for dozen. Across the bottom of the outer betting boxes on each side, you will see three small betting areas marked: "P," "M," and "D." This is where stakes are placed on the first, second and third dozens, respectively. The "P" is short for *première*, or the first 12 numbers. Placing a bet in this outer box is a wager on the numbers 1 through 12. The middle, or *moyen* dozen, numbers 13 through 24, can be wagered by placing a chip in the center box marked "M." A wager on the third dozen (25 through 36) can be accomplished in the area designated with "D," or *derrière* for last 12 numbers. The *douzaines* pay 2 to 1.

Rouge and *noir* are French for red and black. Two of the six large betting areas outside the numbered grid are for betting the *couleurs*. The bottom left box contains a solid black diamond. This is where the players will stake on the *noir*, or black numbers. Its mate, just across the grid on the bottom right side, has the solid red diamond. This area will accommodate wagers on the *rouge*, or red numbers. Each color pays even-money for a win.

Impair and *pair* are the labels used to mark the odd and even betting areas. The *pair*, or even box is on the outer right side-center, just above the black betting area. Any of the even numbers from 2 up to 36 would qualify as a winner. The *impair*, or odd betting area is directly across on the outer left side-center, just above the box for red numbers. These even-money wagers pay 1 to 1.

Passe and *manque* are stakes for high or low numbers. *Passe* is an even-money wager on numbers 19 through 36. Bets are placed in the top left box next to the boxed numbers 1, 4, 7 and 10. Across the grid on the top right, the players can bet on the low, or *manque* numbers (1 through 18). This bet pays 1 to 1.

En prison lines are present in all six outside-wager boxes. This is a broken line that runs parallel with and near the outermost vertical border of the entire betting area on each side. Although the name has a negative connotation, this actually provides a nice option for the even-money bettors. If a chip is staked on an even-money wager and the zero comes in, then the chip is not necessarily lost right away. It is placed "in prison," or on the en prison line corresponding to that betting area. If the 18-numbered group that was bet upon hits on the next spin, then the bet is returned (with no winnings) to the player. If the opposing 18-numbered group results, then it is lost. This effectively cuts the 2.7 percent edge to 1.35 percent on the even-money wagers in Europe. If another zero should appear, then the chip is placed on the outermost border (double in prison) and the bet is returned or lost on the next decision. In Atlantic City, where the surrender option is employed, the casinos settle right away and will immediately return half of your even-money wager if the zeroes appear. The result is the same for either option—the edge is reduced in half for the even-money bets.

Methods of Cheating

Conniving Casinos

Before Nevada legalized gambling in 1931, methods for cheating the patrons were commonly employed. Illegal gambling and other illicit activities were prevalent in Vegas since the turn of the century. Special or modified roulette wheels were part of the action. Many of these rigged, or gaffed wheels remained in operation for several years after 1931. Once the new gaming commission was established and put into power, these wheels found their way over to obscure locations or illegal out-of-state operations. As the Casino Control Commission developed some teeth in its bite, casino cheating decreased to almost nothing in Nevada. When gaming commissioners can stroll up unannounced, confiscate any gaming equipment as they see fit and take it back to their labs for a thorough inspection, the casinos do not want to risk losing their gaming license because of rigged games. Why should they when they have the edge to begin with anyway?

Today, in Nevada or Atlantic City or Mississippi and parts in between, you won't find any gaffed or juiced wheels out on the casino floors. However, any gaming establishment operating where gambling is illegal is already breaking the law and with no license to lose, has no incentive to give a sucker an even break. Be advised, in illegal gaming houses you are probably being cheated in some way. Even in venues where gambling is legal, but where there is no strong regulatory agency, be wary. Here are some of the more common modes of cheating at roulette. Most of these are antiquated, but knowing about them can't hurt you.

Magnets

Probably the most elaborate way to cheat the players in the past was by installing four equally spaced, concealed electromagnets around the stationery bowl. This was used in conjunction with a ball containing a steel core. By activating the magnetic force, a ball could be repelled off the upper race, or ball track and sent down, a little earlier than gravity would dictate, toward the spinning rotor. By pressing a hidden button (thus completing the circuit to the magnets at the appropriate time) a skilled dealer could force the ball drop-off and anticipate a rendezvous with a particular sector of the slowly spinning rotor. The dealer, having sufficiently memorized the wheel layout, could observe the betting layout, target a sparsely wagered sector on the rotor and competently steer the ball away from the heavily bet numbers.

Another method includes using a rotor where certain pockets have been magnetized. Here, a ball with a steel core is spun and allowed to break naturally from the upper track.

As it spirals towards the rotor, it is attracted to the magnetized pockets. Because the rotor is a moving component, it is difficult to devise a way to toggle the charge on and off, so the pockets must be pre-selected and magnetized. If no one had bet on the magnetized numbers, then the dealer would use the steel-cored ball, knowing it would be attracted to these pockets. If there were sufficient action on the magnetized numbers, then the dealer would simply switch back to a regular roulette ball and let the 5.26 percent edge take effect.

Wheel Tampering

The casinos weren't the only ones altering the wheels. There are many stories of brazen individuals who snuck into the casino wheel room after closing and doctored up the roulette wheels. Armed with pliers or other tools, these people would loosen up a few of the pocket frets by twisting them back and forth. These loosened separators would then absorb more of the ball's energy, causing it to remain in that pocket. Others would glue some kind of material to the bottoms of certain pockets to affect the ball's bounce. Depending upon the material, different results could be expected. For example, gluing thin sheets of lead on the bottoms of select pockets would deaden the ball's bounce and make it more likely for the ball to stay in that pocket. Whereas affixing thin sheets of hyper elastic material, like that found in a super ball, to the pocket's bottom would cause the ball to easily bounce out and avoid that particular pocket. Either way, the perpetrator is attempting to create a biased wheel. We'll talk more about biased wheels in **Part 3** and **Part 4**.

Ball Tripping

An easy way to rig a wheel is by ball tripping. A very small diameter hole is drilled in the upper ball track under the rim. A small, spring-loaded pin is positioned in the hole just below the outside surface. This mechanism is usually set up directly in front of the dealer so it is easier for him to time and harder for anyone else to detect. When the dealer flips a small lever, just under the table's edge, the tension in the cable forces the pin against the spring, allowing it to protrude out slightly onto the ball track. As the ball contacts the pin, it is prematurely tripped out of the ball track. Again, a well-practiced dealer would time the ball drop-off with an impending sector of the wheel head or rotor. Because there is only one trip location from which to knock the ball, the dealer must wait for the right ball/trip point/wheel intersection. A near-perfect alignment is necessary and the dealer must see it coming well ahead of time.

The casinos weren't the only ones engaging in this technique. One story has a team of players in Nevada, called The Soda Straw Gang, tapping into the table's banks with a most peculiar method of ball tripping. The gang allegedly had one heavy bettor at the center of the table, one trivial bettor on the far end and an observer seated at the wheel itself. The members would take their stations at different times, being careful not to acknowledge each other. The heavy bettor would cover numbers contained on one sector of the wheel head. Just before the ball would fall, the low-roller on the end would create a diversion. The observer, timing the ball and the heavily bet sector on the wheel, would then raise a straw and blow on the ball as it passed to trip it out of the upper track. Supposedly, the gang was so successful that the casinos began installing the now-present glass security shields around the edge of the roulette tables. Now, don't form a team, buy a box of straws and look for tables without the security shield. If the bosses don't immediately catch you, the cameras most certainly will.

Another tripping technique that I have personally witnessed involves one heavy bettor placing a black chip on the second column and a confederate standing near the wheel. As the ball slowed down, the observer would brace himself and look for an opportunity to manifest. Since the table was filled with last-second bettors all trying to position their chips, there was a lot of bumping going on. As the ball slowed down, and the second column area (concentrated on an area of the rotor centered about the number 26 on an American double-zero wheel) of the wheel approached, the tripper would thrust his hip firmly into the table near the wheel. The nudge seemed to shock the ball momentarily and then it broke from the upper track. Unfortunately for the trippers, that momentary pause let some of the wheel spin by and the ball resultantly bounced beyond their sector. On the next attempt, the tripper thrust more firmly and a little earlier. The ball came down around the 33 and dribbled into the 14, a second-column number. The force of the bump brought unpleasant comments from the other players and a glare from the dealer. Feeling uneasy, the tripper departed. It was then that I noticed the black chip bettor on the end. He collected his winnings and left the table as well. They were lucky that the dealer didn't alert security or that the losing patrons didn't lynch them.

Past Posting

Probably the most common form of player cheating and the easiest to attempt is a method called past posting. This technique originated at the racetracks some years back. As soon as a winning horse was evident (well in the lead), the bettor would hurry to the ticket window and place a bet on that horse. Likewise with roulette, when the ball comes in for its final landing, the dealer will look down for a moment to see what the winning number is. At that instant, a player with a keen eye and adroit hand can place or move his bet to the winning number. Games run by one dealer are most susceptible to this form of chicanery. The cheat may remove losing bets in part or in whole, place winning bets, or switch losers onto the winning number.

One example would be a right-handed player standing at the center of the table and betting on black. Of the even-money wagers, black and red are the only ones that are adjacent to each other. If black comes in, then great; he'll relax and wait for his pay off. But if red comes up, he'll lean over the table and very quickly and precisely tap his bet from black over to red in a fraction of a second. This stratagem requires nerves of steel and a quick, cunning and concise maneuver. The dealers and pit are well aware of this cheating technique and are watching for it. The first time you get caught, you might escape by claiming ignorance. You didn't hear the dealer say "no more bets." After that, you're asking for a RFB comp to the local prison!

Ball Control

Although no casino will admit to its existence and very few dealers will nod in acknowledgment, this method is real, powerful and easy to disguise. One cannot deny that a roulette event is heavily influenced by a human dealer. After all, it is the dealer who kicks up the rotor speed and launches the little white ball isn't it? These actions definitely affect where the ball will land. And after years of repeatedly spinning, the dealer develops what athletes call muscle memory, or a consistent delivery system. As someone who has dealt the game of roulette, I will admit it to you right here: Some dealers can consciously influence the result of the game!

There, I said it!

I know that deflectors may knock a ball off its original course, or that the ball may spatter when it crosses onto the rotor and hits a pocket fret, but even if a skilled dealer could navigate around the heavily bet sectors on the wheel only 10 percent of the time, the casino's edge would be 100 percent for those spins. The house's edge with such a dealer would then be [(9) x 5.26 percent + (1) x 100.00 percent all divided by 10]—a whopping 14.73 percent! To further add to this dilemma, there is no way to prove that the dealer is trying to cheat you, unless you can read minds.

My personal observations have led me to believe that male roulette dealers are more territorial. If you begin to win steadily at their tables, they feel challenged and may spin against you, that is unless you're a shapely female wearing a low-cut dress. I've also seen first-generation immigrants working as dealers, who are staunchly loyal to their new employers. If the issue of ball control troubles you, you can simply wait for the dealer to spin before placing your bets. I also recommend you pay close attention to the section on dealer's signature found in **Part 5**. You can actually turn this technique in your favor. I'll show you how to recognize a skillful dealer, build a rapport with him and exploit his ability.

Concealed Computers

This method involves assessing the mechanical conditions of the roulette event and rendering a computer prediction based on the laws of Newtonian physics. This technique would have appeared in **Part 4** of this book as an advantage system, except that using a computing device to project the outcome of a casino game is illegal in most places. *The Eudaemonic Pie* by Thomas Bass chronicles the adventures and misadventures of Doyne Farmer and Norman Packard, two classmates of Bass's from the University of California at Santa Cruz. These PhDs in physics formed a team with other physicists and computer scientists for the purpose of creating a computer capable of predicting casino roulette. Back in the late 1970s when they endeavored to do this, no law was in place to prohibit the use of computers in a casino. So I want to clarify that technically, Farmer and Packard's attempts to use a concealed computer were not illegal then—but today they would be.

The team designed and built a miniature computer from scratch, since one was not commercially available at the time. They developed and burned in their own software for calculating the various equations of motion involved; such factors as the position, velocity and deceleration of the ball, the proper relationship of the exponentially decaying ball speed and the more constant angular velocity of the wheel head. Because the event always took place on a 32" casino-regulation roulette wheel and the acceleration due to gravity on the Earth's surface is fairly constant, a set of idealized equations of motion were derived for a theoretically perfect roulette wheel.

As they discovered along the way, no two roulette wheels were made, maintained or set up the same way; they adapted their software to have a flexible enough program so that specific characteristics of each roulette wheel could be input. Once the computer had enough background on a certain wheel, it could begin to make adjustments in the algorithms to compensate for these idiosyncrasies.

One such wheel characteristic is the ball's drop-off point from the upper track. If you use the eight silver deflectors in the approach to mentally divide the bowl up into octants, you can chart a histogram of ball drops per octant. Ideally, the ball should be able to drop from any octant, based on when the gravitational acceleration overcomes the centripetal acceleration holding it in the upper track. But this will not happen if the entire wheel is sufficiently tilted at say, 1/8" to 1/4". The ball will labor as it climbs the incline toward the tilt's apex, slowing it down more than expected. This is where the ball will tend to run out of gas so to speak. I've seen wheels where 45 percent of the drop-offs occurred in just one octant. Chances are that the drop-off octant was at or just before the tilt's highest point. If the ball should make it over the peak, it will accelerate slightly as it races down the other side. This uncharacteristic slowing and speeding up may not be perceptible to the human eye, but it is enough to throw off any idealized mathematical model.

Farmer and Packard's team did an excellent job of interpreting the problem and programming it into their custom computer, but there were logistical problems; difficulty concealing the computer and its power supply, loose wires, bad connections, shocks, clamping solenoids, drifting signals, etc. Building such a device involved extensive knowledge of physics, mathematics, electronics, computer science and information theory. Even after a year and a half of totally redesigning and miniaturizing their system with the latest technology available, they were overcome by unexpected computer crashes and electronic noise. This noise came from surveillance systems and low-frequency radiation given off by neon signs and slot machines. These all contributed spurious signals to the receiver. The casinos are a swamp of electronic noise and the roulette team was sinking in the electromagnetic mire.

Then in 1985, just as our team of physicists was contemplating their next go-around, the Governor of Nevada signed Senate Bill 467 into law. The pertinent statute in Nevada states: "It is unlawful for any person at a licensed gaming establishment to use, or possess with the intent to use, any device to assist in projecting the outcome of the game." The statute goes on to say that a first-time offender may be imprisoned for a period of 1 to 10 years, or be fined up to $10,000, or both. A second offense is mandatory imprisonment. In other words, if you're caught with a computer in the casino, even if you did not yet use it, you may be hit with jail time and stiff fines. New Jersey has a similar statute regarding the use of electronic, electrical and mechanical devices: "Except as specifically permitted by the commission, no person shall possess with the intent to use, or actually use, at any table game, either by himself or in concert with others, any calculator, computer or other electronic, electrical or mechanical device to assist in projecting an outcome at any table game or in keeping track of or analyzing the cards having been dealt, the changing probabilities of any table game, or the playing strategies to be utilized."

As computers become smaller, they are also becoming more powerful, reliable and more programmer-friendly. The temptations of easy riches become greater. There are still those scheming to build computers for predicting roulette, despite the fact that doing so could result in disaster for the users. I recently ran across this ad on the Internet:

ROULETTE PHYSICS
WANTED!! INVESTORS/SPONSORS
POCKET-SIZED ROULETTE COMPUTER
USES PREDICTIVE PHYSICS/MECHANICS

This is NOT a betting scheme. Computer has proven advantage over the casino of 15–30 percent daily. Capable of predicting approximate final position of ball. Capital required for profiting tour of casinos. Send contact details and all inquires for information.

My advice would be to steer clear of these groups unless you're looking to spend an extended vacation with them!

Slick Surveillance

Although the casinos have always had the home court advantage, that hasn't stopped the ne'er-do-wells from attempting to cheat the house. In the past, panels of one-way glass were installed in the ceilings over the casino floor. Surveillance people, often referred to as the eye in the sky, would tread back and forth on narrow catwalks while looking down at the games. With binoculars in hand, they monitored both the players and the dealers for any signs of cheating. They maneuvered through spider webs and around posts and rafters in the dark. Today's modern casinos are outfitted with hundreds of cameras that can rotate, pivot and zoom in

on a pinhead. These cameras are housed in those half-spheri-
cal bubbles that you see, mounted from the ceiling. They send
video signals that are fed into dozens of monitors with videotapes rolling.

However, not all of the cameras' signals can be shown
on a monitor at all times. Just because the camera is on does-
n't mean that someone is watching it. The video can later be
reviewed, but the cheat or thief may be long gone by then.
The surveillance crew must switch back and forth between
cameras, focusing more on the busy betting areas and the
cashiers' cages. If the pit is suspicious of a cheat, or if a high
roller steps into the game, the boss will call up to surveillance
to make sure they are watching the action at that table.

Eventually, the whole system will be computerized. A
network of several hundred tiny digital cameras will be
mounted throughout the casino. As these cameras sense
movement, they will begin processing a digital signal to a
computer. Surveillance software will interpret any actions it
senses and the most questionable of those will appear on one
of several main monitors where a small surveillance crew will
be stationed. Because the footage is digital and fully indexed,
it can be immediately accessed and cross-referenced with
other footage taken, even if it happened six months earlier.
There will be no archived tapes to search through, no hours
and hours of rewinding and playing of videotapes.
Everything will be stored in one central database. Big brother
will be watching and he'll never forget a face!

Part 2

What It Takes to Win in the Long Run

Mathematical Systems

Systems, systems, systems . . . everyone wants a good mathematical system to employ at the tables. Many roulette enthusiasts who visit my website have given me the details of systems that they are currently playing and have asked me to analyze them, which I have done. Unfortunately, there are no good mathematical betting systems in existence . . . only bad, very bad and awful systems. Nevertheless, before I get too far into this discussion, let me help define what a betting or mathematical system is.

A mathematical system is a scheme by which the amount of your next wager is determined by what happened on your last bet. Raise after a loss, raise after a win, or some convoluted method of tracking sequences of losses or wins to formulate subsequent wagers is a betting or mathematical system. The mathematical system pays absolutely no credence whatsoever to the physical conditions that caused the outcome. It does not even account for which game you are playing. No matter how great a betting system you believe that you have, one thing is for certain. On the American double-zero roulette wheel there are 38 pockets and the casino only pays you 35 to 1. What does this mean? That means that you are taxed on your winnings and not your losses. Losing is free, so to speak. If the game were fair, you would receive 37 to 1 on a straight up win and 18 to 1 on a split, for example. You are always paid as if there were 36 pockets instead of 38. This is how the house is able to run a thriving business. Please realize that a system based purely on whether or not you won a previous bet will lose your bankroll over a sustained period.

The House Edge

Let us calculate the house edge for any roulette wager. First, you will take the actual payoff minus the correct payoff. Now multiply that by the probability of hitting your number. Multiply that by 100 to convert to a percentage and you come out with the house edge that the casinos bank on:

$[35/1 - 37/1] \times 1/38 \times 100\% = 5.263$ percent *against* the player.

Incidentally, the edge on the single-zero wheel is similarly calculated, but remember that we are only shorted one unit instead of two. In addition, the probability of hitting is one chance in 37. Therefore, we have:

$[35/1 - 36/1] \times 1/37 \times 100\% = 2.703$ percent *against* the player.

"Yeah, but I have this new betting system that I just bought," you might say. "The seller unconditionally guarantees that I will win 96 percent (or some impressive percentage) of the time!" I will show you that these claims, while technically correct, are also seriously misleading.

The Due Theory

Most betting systems would have you wager on some number or group of numbers. A group of numbers could be the red or odd numbers, or the second column numbers, or the 1 through 6 line, etc. Usually, you are instructed to increase the amount of your next bet based on something impressive called "The Maturity of Chances" or "The Law of Large Numbers." Those who know better refer to this as "The Gambler's Fallacy." The endorsers of these *due* systems will have you believe that sooner or later, your group has to come in—after all, if the event hasn't happened in awhile it is due to happen, right? Well, such reasoning is true over the long run; but the happening in the short run could be sooner but it also could be later . . . much, much later at times. Over the course of 50,000 spins, the chances of, say, the number 8 not occurring for 150 spins in a row would not even register a *hiccup* in the overall statistical scheme of things. You will not have the bankroll necessary (infinite) to execute your "It's due!" betting scheme and, even if you did, the house imposes minimum and maximum bet sizes, so you are limited regardless.

These *due* systems have been around for hundreds of years. They did not work then, and they still do not work today. Anyone who claims that they are selling a newly developed or recently rediscovered betting system is feeding you a line. The seller is attempting to dupe you into thinking that his system is something special . . . something unique, when it is just a re-cooked or warmed-over version of one of the classical systems. It is probably some variation of a Martingale, Labouchere, Fibonacci or d'Alembert system. What tends to happen with any of these betting-based systems is that you may experience a series of small wins, deceptively building a false sense of infallibility. However, as you continue to play, you inevitably will be wiped out by one catastrophic loss . . . and if you are really unfortunate, you could experience that disaster right away or several times in a relatively short span of time.

Another approach is to play a particular system in reverse, sometimes called contra systems. The reasoning here is that if negative progressions don't work, how about trying a positive progression, or an up-as-you-win progression? Let me assure you that this does nothing to change the casino's edge any more than the due systems. The game of roulette just is not a fair game and no due system can ever overcome this fact. I am sure that you have heard the phrase, "The wheel has no memory." In fact, it has no consciousness either, and only a conscious mind would notice the absence of a particular grouping of numbers from the tote boards. Remember that each spin is an *independent* event. The house edge is constant and immutable no matter what has happened in previous spins. On any given trial, any of the 38 possibilities could come up. Also, there is no way to arrange a collection of bets on any given spin in such a way that will produce an expected win over the long haul. Each individual wager will have a negative edge and, as you probably remember from your fourth grade math class, the sum of several negative numbers is just a much larger negative number.

Personal Experience with My Own Betting System

When I first began my adventures in roulette, an idea occurred to me. This is an idea that I'm sure occurred to thousands of other gamblers over the course of time. But, of course, like many of those before me, I thought I had stumbled onto something new. If I were to make the minimum wager on a group of numbers and lose, I would simply up my bet for this same group on the next attempt. Eventually this grouping has to come in. So, I studied the betting layout to see what combinations of wagers could be concocted. I settled on the first dozen bet. I liked the fact that it paid 2 to 1, and I noticed that it was the most evenly distributed number group on the roulette wheel of the dozens or columns bets available. I reasoned that if I were winning big, it would be very difficult for the dealer to try to spin against me. I actually was on to something, but not with the betting system.

I intuitively realized that some dealers do have the ability to *steer* their way around the wheel, and I started to look at how the wheel itself was laid out. In the following sections, you will see just how important these two concepts are to predictive playing. Anyway, the system that I discovered was just a variation of the old Martingale. Many a family fortune was lost at the tables because of this system. With a simple Martingale, the losing bettor would increase his next wager by the inverse of the payoff. Hence, someone betting on an outside bet (red or black, even or odd, high or low) would be paid 1 to 1. The inverse of $1/1$ is 1, so you would increase your bet by one unit (double up). For the dozens or columns group the payoff is 2 to 1, so you would invert $2/1$ and get $1/2$. You would increase your next wager by $1/2$, or 50 percent, in order to win the same original amount.

Surfing the First Dozen

Let us say that you placed a $10 bet on the first dozen and won. You would be returned the original $10 wager plus $20 in winnings, or 2 to 1. Now let's say that you lost that same $10 wager. You would increase your bet 50 percent and wager a $15 sum on the first dozen. If you won this bet, you would net $30, which covers the first $10 bet that you made, plus a net-net winning of the original $20 that you had hoped to win. Because we have to work in increments of $5, we cannot always increase the bet by exactly 50 percent, but it is close enough to keep a good account of things. If you had lost the $15 bet, you would have to choose between $20 and $25 for your next progression since you cannot bet $22.50 for an outside wager at the roulette table. The inverse progression rule works for all other bet types on the baize. You can work the other ones out for yourself.

Using any of the dozens or columns bets, let me show you how sellers of systems can accurately make claims that their system will win, for example, 85 percent of the time. This success percentage can be adjusted up or down depending on the particular bet's probability of hitting and the maximum number of successive bets chosen for the losing progression.

Mutual Exclusivity

Okay, let us briefly review a few probabilistic laws to help clarify things. When you place a wager in roulette, one of two events may occur on that trial. Either the bet is a winner or it is a loser. One of these decisions must occur to be considered a bet. That is to say that the events defined as winning or losing are mutually exclusive. In addition, on subsequent trials, the probability of winning or losing remains constant. Unlike blackjack, where cards are removed from play (put in the discard pile), roulette is a game of replacements. Just because the number 5 comes up on one spin, it is not removed from the wheel for the next spin. The number 5 has the exact same probability of winning on any given trial. Each trial is independent of the ones that preceded it.

For mutually exclusive events, the probabilities of either winning or losing add up to 1. So:

$P(Win) + P(Loss) = 1$

i.e., $P(first dozen win) + P(first dozen lose) = 1$

or, $12/38 + 26/38 = 1$

For any bet that you can make on the baize, you will either win or lose, and the respective probabilities will always add up to 1. This satisfies all of the conditions to qualify as a binomial distribution problem. When we analyze the probability of winning over a series of some number of trials, we can simply multiply the probabilities of each independent trial together to get the probability of at least one win during a cycle of progressive bets. Let me help clarify this with an example:

What is the probability of tossing at least one head in three attempts for an evenly balanced coin? We know that the chance of success is 50-50 or P(Win) = 1/2 and P(Loss) = 1/2.

We must calculate the following probabilities:

P(W) = win on first toss = P(W) = 1/2

P(L,W) = win on second toss = P(L) x P(W) =
          (1/2) x (1/2) = 1/4

P(L,L,W) = win on third toss = P(L) x P(L) x P(W) =
          (1/2) x (1/2) x (1/2) = 1/8

Now we will sum up all of the probabilities:

P(W) + P(L,W) + P(L,L,W) = 1/2 + 1/4 + 1/8 = 7/8

The probability of throwing at least one head in three attempts is 7/8. Conversely, the probability of failing to throw any heads in three attempts is 1 – 7/8 = 1/8 (12.5 percent of the time). We could have easily calculated this using the multiplicative rule as follows:

P(L,L,L) = (1/2) x (1/2) x (1/2) = 1/8 and 1 – 1/8 = 7/8

Let's say that I am willing to make five attempts to win the first-dozen bet. What is the chance that I will lose all five bets? What is the chance that I will win at least one bet?

P(L,L,L,L,L) = (26/38)5 = 0.14995 or 15 percent

1 – P(L,L,L,L,L) = P(W), or 1 – .15 = .85

Therefore, there is an 85 percent chance that I will win one bet in that cycle. Incidentally, this is how the system sellers are able to make such claims. I reasoned that if I had an 85 percent chance of success, I would simply increase my next wager (losing progression) until I won. Using the inverse payoff formula, I would only need one win in any given cycle to net two initial units. I thought: I must be a genius!

So, I ventured out into the casino. Unable to contain my excitement, I also got my brother-in-law very fired up about this. We each started with a bankroll of $700. We agreed to surf the first dozens using the following losing progression: $25, $35, $50, $75 and finally $115. If we won a bet, then we would start the progression at $25 again. If we lost our fifth bet of $115, we would attempt a new cycle or call the session.

The Revelation

For any given cycle, we had an 85 percent chance of winning as much as $50. We had found the golden goose . . . or so we thought. A funny thing did happen in the beginning, though. We began to win . . . and win . . . and win some more. In fact, we were winning about 10 out of every 11 cycles. We were riding an incredible streak of good luck. In the back of my mind, I knew we were living on borrowed time. A little voice kept saying, "Hey, genius, every bet that you're making has a negative edge. How long do you think you can keep this up?" I knew it was too good to last so I calculated the expected return for this system. The calculation went as follows:

First, we have to calculate the probability that a certain event will occur. We will do this for all of the possible events, given a progression of five potential wagers:

$P(W) = (12/38) = 0.3158 . . .$

or a 31.58 percent chance of success on the first attempt.

$P(L, W) = (26/38) \times (12/38) = 0.2161 . . .$

or a 21.61 percent chance of success of one loss and then a win.

$P(L, L, W) = (26/38)^2 \times (12/38) = 0.1478 . . .$

or a 14.78 percent chance of having two loses, then a win.

P(L, L, L, W) = $(26/38)^3$ x $(12/38)$ = 0.1011 . . .

> or a 10.11 percent chance of success after exactly three losses.

P(4 L, W) = $(26/38)^4$ x $(12/38)$ = 0.0692 . . .

> or a 6.92 percent chance of seeing four losses followed by a win.

P(5 Losses) = $(26/38)^5$ = 0.1500 . . .

> for a 15 percent chance of failure

Total probability of all events = 1.0000 . . . or 100 percent

Next, we compute the expected dollars for each of the possible events. We accomplish this by multiplying the probabilities of each event times the payoff or loss of each event:

Expected $(W) =

$$(2 \times \$25) \times 0.3158 = +\$15.79$$

Expected $(L, W) =

$$[(2 \times \$35) - \$25] \times 0.2161 = +\$9.72$$

Expected $(L, L, W) =

$$[(2 \times \$50) - (\$35 + \$25)] \times 0.1478 = +\$5.91$$

Expected $(L, L, L, W) =

$$[(2 \times \$75) - (\$50 + \$35 + \$25)] \times 0.1011 = +\$4.04$$

Expected $(4 L, W) =

$$[(2 \times \$115) - (\$75 + \$50 + \$35 + \$25)] \times 0.0692 = +\$3.11$$

Expected $(5 Losses) =

$$[-(\$25 + \$35 + \$50 + \$75 + \$115)] \times 0.1500 = -\$45.00$$

Total expected dollars for each cycle played = –$6.43

I couldn't believe it. After three months and some 500+ cycles of play, I should have been drawn down over $3,215. That's 128+ units! Amazingly, I was ahead $7,800! And my more aggressive brother-in-law was up $9,600!! I remember an icy chill going up my spine. At that moment, I resolved to stop using mathematically based staking systems for games of independent trials.

Unfortunately, I was not able to convince my brother-in-law of our incredibly lucky streak. He believed that the system was responsible for our success. Fortunately for me, I banked my profits before ruination and went back to the drawing board. My stubborn brother-in-law continued to surf the first dozen . . . it didn't take long, maybe a month, but he had given back everything he made times three! The fantasy was over and reality reared its ugly head. Everything was back in a state of equilibrium.

As a side note, I discovered that someone was selling almost the exact same system I just described in one of the more popular gaming periodicals for $295. They were claiming an 85 percent win rate and I verified that they were recommending that you select any one of the dozens or columns bets and play a negative progression five bets deep.

There is an expression a seasoned veteran and good friend of mine uses called The Superman Complex. It describes how I felt before I crunched all the numbers; and for the way my brother-in-law felt right up to the bitter end. It is a feeling like the only thing that can harm you is kryptonite. The problem with most systems is that many times you will experience a series of little wins before the inevitable happens. Unfortunately, these little wins build up a false sense of confidence and that is the last thing that you want to have. Such a blissful sleep of ignorance will result in having your head handed to you. If you are fortunate enough to get ahead using a betting-based or mathematical system, you will have to suck in your ego, open up your eyes and admit that luck, not skill is responsible for your current state.

Let us go on to discuss the most widely used of these systems in detail.

The Martingale

Probably the most popular system of them all is the Martingale. It is most likely as old as gambling itself. The Martingale system has you increasing your wager after a loss . . . the old double or nothing routine. You continue to increase your bets in an up-as-you-lose fashion until you finally do win. At that point, you begin the progression all over again. Your objective is to win one unit, usually on the even-money wagers. If it were a fair game, you would not get hurt in the long run using this system, as you would break even.

Let us assume that the casino was feeling generous, so they removed the zeroes from the rotor and left the payouts the same. You are there and decide to wager on red up to five times in a row, in order to hit at least once. Your betting progression would look like this:

1. Bet $5 on red. If you win, then start a new progression and repeat step 1. If you lose (50 percent chance for a fair game), go to step 2.

2. Now bet $10 on red. A win here takes you back to step 1. A loss takes you up to step 3. There is a 25 percent chance of losing the first two bets.

3. Bet $20 on red. If you hit, go back to step 1. If you lose your third bet (a 12.5 percent chance), go on to step 4.

4. Bet $40 on red. A win has you start a new progression. A loss will have you go on to step 5. The chances of losing four straight are 6.25 percent.

5. Now bet $80 on red. A win puts you back at step 1. A loss also puts you back at step 1 (or at the ATM machine). At this point, you have lost the whole progression. The chance of losing the whole series is 1 in 32, which is 3.125 percent of the time.

You will note that if you win at any time during the progression, you will be ahead $5 or one basic betting unit.

You will have won that progression and will attempt a new one. Because the zeroes were removed (a fair game), your chances of winning $5 in the first step are exactly 1/2. Your chances of losing $5 are therefore 1/2 also. The chances that you will lose steps 1 and 2 are $(1/2)^2$, or $(1/2) \times (1/2) = 1/4$. The chances of losing the first three steps are $(1/2)^3 = 1/8$, for a 1 in 8 chance. Following this down through step 4 (1 in 16 chance), and finally at step 5, the probability of losing the whole series is $(1/2)^5 = 1/32$, or 3.125 percent of the time. That means you will win the progression 96.875 percent of the time. "That's virtually a lock!" you say. But let's take a closer look.

If I played 32 cycles of the progression, I will win my 1 unit 31 out of 32 attempts or 96.875 percent of the time. So, 31 x $5 = $155, not bad. However, I will lose the whole series one time in 32, or 3.125 percent of the time. This means 1 x ($5 + $10 + $20 + $40 + $80) = –$155.

That works out to dead even as $155 – $155 = $0. That's why we would call it a fair game. By the way, the length of the betting progression has no bearing here on the consequences . . . longer or shorter, it still breaks even. Over the long haul, the person betting on this fair game will not get hurt.

Let's say that the casino was not making any money offering a fair game, so they added the two zeroes back in, but kept the payouts the same. The progression will look the same, but the chances of winning are reduced. We now have 20 ways to lose out of 38 numbers:

1. $5 on red. You will now lose 20/38, or 52.63 percent instead of 50 percent of the time.

2. $10 on red. Now loses you $(20/38)^2$, or 27.70 percent instead of 25 percent of the time.

3. $20 on red. You lose $(20/38)^3$, or 14.58 percent of the time instead of 12.5 percent.

4. $40 on red. You will lose $(20/38)^4$, or 7.67 percent instead of 6.25 percent of the time.

5. $80 on red. You now lose $(20/38)^5$, or 4.04 percent instead of 3.125 percent of the time.

"So I lose a little less than one percent more often," one might say. "What's the big deal?" Let's look at the unfair game more closely:

In 32 cycles, you will now win only 95.96 percent instead of 96.875 percent of your wagers. So, 0.9596 x 32 x $5 = 30.707 x $5 = $153.54. "Not too far off from the $155, previously," one might be quick to point out.

But, you will see we are losing much more . . . 0.0404 x 32 x $155 = 1.2928 x $155 = –$200.38!

By the way, you now know how a system can win 96 percent of the time (as claimed in some sales ads) and still lose money overall. The systems sellers forget to mention that the one disastrous loss on average will, over the long run, wipe out all of your winnings, plus some. The calculation above shows our net loss is $153.54 – $200.38 = –$46.84. This is the average you will lose over 32 cycles of playing this progression. "Wow, I'm losing one percent more often and I'm averaging –$46.84 over 32 attempts . . . I know, I'll just increase the progression to six bets! That should more than pick up that extra one percent," one could reason.

Well, let's see.

6. Now raise bet to $160 on red after five straight losses. This bet will lose $[20/38]^6$, or only 2.13 percent of the time! Great!

Hold on, the judges are conferring . . .

In 32 cycles, you will win 97.87 percent of your wagers. So, (0.9787) x 32 x $5 = 31.318 x $5 = $156.59.

But, you are losing (0.0213) x 32 x ($5+ $10+ $20+ $40+ $80+ $160) = 0.6816 x $315 = –$214.70!

That means $156.59 – $214.70 = –$58.11, for a net loss of $58.11 every 32 cycles on average. "I'm losing 24 percent more money by extending the progression from five to six! Let's shorten it down to four instead," you correctly conclude. Now you are on the right track. The longer your progression in an unfair game, the more you will lose with that progression. Remember, you are exposing larger amounts to that house edge on the back end of your progression. It is simple really—the more that you bet, the more you will lose.

Using our calculations from above we can determine what our expected loss will be on a four-bet progression. We notice that we will lose $5 + $10 + $20 + $40 = $75. This will happen 7.67 percent of the time. So, we see (0.9233) x 32 x $5 = $147.73 in average winnings and (0.0767) x 32 x $75 = $184.08 in loses. Our resulting net loss has been reduced to $36.35! If you follow the mathematics all the way down to a progression of zero bets, then you will reduce the losses down to $0.

The Grand Martingale

One notable variation to the Martingale is the Grand Martingale. The only thing "grand" about this system is the fashion in which you will lose your money. This more aggressive cousin has you double your last bet and add one more unit. If our betting unit were $5, then the progression would look like this:

1. $5 on red. You lose (20/38), or 52.63 percent of the time, and win 47.37 percent of the time.

2. $10 + $5 on red. You lose $(20/38)^2$, or 27.70 percent and win 72.30 percent of the time.

3. $30 + $5 on red. You lose $(20/38)^3$, or 14.58 percent of the time, and win 85.42 percent.

4. $70 + $5 on red. Will have you losing $(20/38)^4$, or 7.67 percent, and winning 92.33 percent of the time.

5. $150 + $5 on red. You now lose $[20/38]^5$, or 4.04 percent, and win 95.96 percent of the time.

The "grand" total that you are prepared to lose on just one progression with this system is [$5 + $15 + $35 + $75 + $155] = $285. Let us calculate our average net loss for the same 32 cycles of the progression:

1. [18/38] or 47.37 percent of the time, in 32 attempts, we will win $5: (0.4737) x 32 x $5 = +$75.79

2. [(20/38) x 18/38] or 24.93 percent of our 32 cycles, we will win $10: (0.2493) x 32 x $10 = +$79.78

3. [(20/38)^2 x 18/38], 13.12 percent of our 32 tries, we will win $15: (0.1312) x 32 x $15 = +$62.98

4. [(20/38)^3 x 18/38], 6.91 percent of our 32 attempts will win us $20: (0.0691) x 32 x $20 = +$44.22

5. [(20/38)^4 x 18/38], 3.63 percent of our 32 cycles will win $25: (0.0363) x 32 x $25 = +$29.04

That leaves (20/38)^5 or 4.04 percent of the time for losing $285: (0.0404) x 32 x $285 = –$368.45

Net Loss: $76.64

Therefore, this five-bet progression loses $76.64 in "grand" style versus the more modest $46.84 for the plain Martingale. The Grand loses 63.6 percent more money on a five-bet progression. This system is deadly, folks. Stay clear.

The d'Alembert

Another popular mathematical system is named after Jean Le Rond d'Alembert, a French mathematician and physicist who was born in 1717. His theory on the Law of Equilibrium supposes a balance of successes and failures of certain events if you consider a long series of these events. His theory was misapplied to a betting system based on a much shorter span of casino outcomes. The d'Alembert, sometimes referred to as the Pyramid System, has you increase your bet

by one unit after a loss and decrease your bet by one unit after
a win. One typical sequence would be handled as follows:

1. Bet 1 unit	Lose,	–1 unit
2. Up to 2 units	Win,	+1 unit
3. Bet 1 unit	Lose,	+0 units
4. Up to 2 units	Lose,	–2 units
5. Up to 3 units	Win,	+1 unit
6. Bet 2 units	Win,	+3 units

Your unit can be equal to $1, $5, $25 or anything that
you designate. If your unit were $5, then you would be down
$5 after the first wager. Your second stake is $10 and the win
puts you up to a net of one unit, or $5. Now you decrease
your next bet after a win, back to $5. The loss of $5 puts you
even at zero units. The next bet of two units loses so you
increase to three units. Because you win this wager, you will
now decrease your stake to two units. This wager wins and
you are up a total of three units thus far. There is no determined stop-win point with the system, so you must set one
for yourself. If a one-unit profit were fine for you, then you
would have won the sequence after the second wager (being
up one unit) and quit or began a new sequence. If two or three
units were your objective, then the sixth bet would have suf-
ficed. The higher your objective win, the longer the sequence
will be. You should also pre-select a stop-loss point for any
sequence that you play to help control losses. Notice that this
sequence has three wins and three losses. When the wins and
losses balance each other, or are in equilibrium, then your net
gain is equal to the number of wins in your sequence. This
sequence has three wins that balance out three losses. The net
gain is three units.

Aside from the stop-win and stop-loss points, you will
need to determine what size unit you will use and how many
units you will start with. Let's look at the same sequence, but
we will start with five units this time:

1. Bet 5 units	Lose,	−5 units
2. Up to 6 units	Win,	+1 unit
3. Bet 5 units	Lose,	−4 units
4. Up to 6 units	Lose,	−10 units
5. Up to 7 units	Win,	−3 units
6. Bet 6 units	Win,	+3 units

You will note that the same three units result as our net gain. You will also notice that the fluctuations seem to be wilder with the second sequence (−10 units versus −2 units). This happened mainly because we started with a more aggressive five-unit wager for the second progression and the first loss right out of the gate put us deep in the hole. Let us evaluate another situation involving the same sequence of wins and losses. If our starting bet is the same for both sequences, say $5, then our unit size will be $5 for the first progression and only $1 for the second one. The second progression now becomes the more conservative of the two. The first would be executed as follows:

1. Bet $5 or 1 unit	Lose,	−$5
2. Up to $10 (2 units)	Win,	+$5
3. Bet $5 or 1 unit	Lose,	+$0
4. Up to $10 (2 units)	Lose,	−$10
5. Up to $15, 3 units	Win,	+$5
6. Bet $10 (2 units)	Win,	+$15

The same starting point of $5, but with $1 units instead, would be carried out as follows:

1. Bet $5 or 5 units	Lose,	−$5
2. Up to $6 (6 units)	Win,	+$1
3. Bet $5 or 5 units	Lose,	−$4
4. Up to $6 (6 units)	Lose,	−$10
5. Up to $7 or 7 units	Win,	−$3
6. Bet $6 (6 units)	Win,	+$3

Using the same sequence of wins and loses and the same starting bet of $5, we can obtain vastly different net wins using different unit sizes. Both sequences are drawn down exactly $10 after the fourth wager and the wins are equal to the unit size times the number of wins. The actual winning dollar amount, however, is different. The more aggressive first version with the larger size unit wins $15. Compare that to a mere $3 win for the second progression using a $1 unit size on the same sequence of wins and losses.

Do not get too excited though. The more aggressive progression of any system will win more if applied to a winning sequence of events. Please realize that if we had a losing sequence, the more aggressive $5 unit progression will work harder against you, losing money much faster. Because there are more ways to lose than win on an even-money wager (18 wins versus 20 losses out of 38 trials), you will be on the losing side of the sequence more often. I chose to portray a more favorable sequence here as an example. You are better off in the end, losing less with the smaller unit size than winning more with a larger unit size. Let us examine the tree diagram of the d'Alembert system. For this example, we are using a $5 unit and will limit the progression to no more than five wagers.

The tree diagram is called that because it spreads out as it grows, just like a tree, as the possibilities expand. Starting with one wager, you can easily see how all the possibilities develop going up to five bets deep. Once you know what all the possible outcomes are, you can calculate the likelihood of each terminal event on the tree. The terminal events are represented with rounded boxes and contain the probability of reaching that particular outcome. The chances of winning the first bet are easy to see. There are 18 ways out of 38 to win the wager; so 18 divided by 38 equals 0.4737 or 47.37 percent. In order to win after the second bet you would have lost the first, then won the second. The chances of losing the first wager (20/38) multiplied by the chances of winning the sec-

The d'Alembert Tree Diagram

(5-bet progression using a $5 unit)

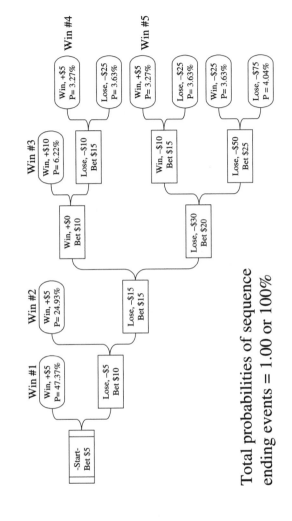

Total probabilities of sequence
ending events = 1.00 or 100%

Diagram 2-A
The d'Alembert Tree Diagram

ond (18/38) are 24.93 percent. To calculate the probability of reaching a particular point on the tree diagram, just count the number of wins and loses along the way and apply them as exponents before multiplying everything together. We can calculate the likelihood of winning a sequence by losing three bets and winning two bets, for example, as in win #5:

P(Lose) x P(Lose) x P(Lose) x P(Win) x P(Win) = P(Win #5), which is the probability that this exact sequence will occur.

If: P(Win) = 18/38 and P(Lose) = 20/38, for each spin, then: $(20/38)^3 \times (18/38)^2 = P(\text{Win #5})$.

P(Win #5) = 0.0327 or 3.27 percent

If you calculate all the probabilities of terminal events and add them together, they should equal 1.00 (or 100 percent). A terminal event is an event that causes the progression to end. A situation where the bettor is ahead after the first through fourth bets would end the progression. After placing the fifth wager, win, lose or draw, we have decided to quit the sequence. Take the amount of money that we are ahead or behind for each terminal event and multiple it times the probability of that event. Now sum these up to calculate the average money won or lost for this particular betting system:

Win #1 ($5):	$8/38 \times \$5$	+$2.37
Win #2 ($5):	$(20/38) \times (18/38) \times \$5$	+$1.25
Win #3 ($5):	$(20/38)^2 \times (18/38)^2 \times \$5$	+$0.62
Win #4 ($5):	$(20/38)^3 \times (18/38)^2 \times \$5$	+$0.16
Win #5 ($5):	$(20/38)^4 \times (18/38)^2 \times \$5$	+$0.16
Average Total Winnings:		**+$4.56**
Lose ($25):	$(20/38)^4 \times (18/38) \times -\$25$	−$0.91
Lose ($25):	$(20/38)^4 \times (18/38) \times -\$25$	−$0.91
Lose ($25):	$(20/38)^4 \times (18/38) \times -\$25$	−$0.91
Lose ($75):	$(20/38)^5 \times -\$75$	−$3.02
Average Total Loses:		**−$5.75**

Allowing up to a five-bet progression with $5 units, the d'Alembert delivers $4.56 in wins and $5.75 in loses, for a net loss of $1.19 per betting sequence. Another useful bit of information is the average number of spins, or bets per progression. The summation of the number of spins times the probability of ending the progression in as many spins gives us this statistic. For the first four bets, the player must win to end the sequence. Otherwise, the sequence is automatically terminated after the fifth bet. You will note, there is no terminal event in the third spin, so the probability of ending the betting progression is zero. Here is how the calculation would look:

P(1 spin) x 1 spin = P(Win #1), or 0.4737 x 1 spin = 0.4737

P(2 spins) x 2 spins = P(Win #2), or 0.2493 x 2 spins = 0.4986

P(3 spins) x 3 spins = 0, or 0.0 x 3 spins = 0.0

P(4 spins) x 4 spins = P(Win #3), or 0.0622 x 4 spins = 0.2488

P(5 spins) x 5 spins = (1.0000 − .7852),
       or 0.2148 x 5 spins = 1.0740

Average number of spins for a five-bet progression = 2.2951,
       or 2.3 spins.

We could have calculated the probability of all six terminal events in the fifth spin and added them together to get the probability of going to five spins. Because these events are mutually exclusive, it is easier to subtract from 1.00 the chances of ending the progression in spins one through four. The probability of ending in spins one through four is [0.4737 +0.2493 +0.0 +0.0622] or 0.7852. Therefore, we have 100 percent minus 78.52 percent, which equals a 21.48 percent chance of ending the progression in the fifth spin. Taking the sum of all probabilities multiplied by the spins needed is about 2.3 average spins per progression for a five-bet d'Alembert. If we lose $1.19 per progression and each progression averages 2.3 spins, then we are expecting a loss of almost 52 cents per bet. I have performed these calculations for the other systems contained in this book, but I've spared you all the mathematical details. This data can be found in **Table 2-C**. If you like, you can verify the other numbers using the d'Alembert calculations as a model.

The Labouchere

The Labouchere system was named for a minister in Queen Victoria's service. Labouchere is credited for using the system although it is not known if he invented it. This betting method, also called the cancellation system, involves some record keeping. The player begins with a series of numbers— any series that he wishes to use. The series chosen will tally up to the number of units that the system player is trying to win. The player begins by betting the sum of the first and last number in the series. If the bettor wins this wager, he will cross out both of these numbers. If he loses, he will add the last bet made to the end of the series. Let's say, for example, that the series used is 1-2-3-4-5-6. If the player is successful in canceling out the entire line, he will win exactly 21 units, or 1 + 2 + 3 + 4 + 5 + 6. Let's play our example out to illustrate the mechanics of this system. The "x" denotes numbers that are canceled out after a winning bet:

Starting Line:	1-2-3-4-5-6	+0 units
1. Bet 1 + 6, or 7 units and win:	x-2-3-4-5-x	+7 units
2. Bet 2 + 5, or 7 units and lose:	x-2-3-4-5-x-7	+0 units
3. Bet 2 + 7, or 9 units and lose:	x-2-3-4-5-x-7-9	–9 units
4. Bet 2 + 9, or 11 units and win:	x-x-3-4-5-x-7-x	+2 units
5. Bet 3 + 7, or 10 units and win:	x-x-x-4-5-x-x-x	+12 units
6. Bet 4 + 5, or 9 units and lose:	x-x-x-4-5-x-x-x-9	+3 units
7. Bet 4 + 9, or 13 units and win:	x-x-x-x-5-x-x-x-x	+16 units
8. Bet 5 units and win:	x-x-x-x-x-x-x-x-x	+21 units

There are a couple of points of interest. First, you will see the 21-unit win that occurs once the line is completely canceled out. Secondly, the bets start off high (7 units in this case) and can escalate quickly (up to 13 units) and this is a "friendly" sequence of wins and losses. Because the 5 is the only number remaining before the last wager, it represents the total bet to be made. If it had lost, then the next wager would have been this 5 plus the 5 added at the end to account for the loss. Each time a wins occurs, two numbers get canceled out, whereas each loss that you experience has you adding only one number to the end of the sequence. This is supposedly the selling point of the system. The series shrinks *two* numbers for a win, but only grows *one* number for a loss. The proponents forget to mention that the one number added is equal to the last bet which was the sum of two numbers. Therefore, you are trading one larger number for the removal of two smaller numbers. Let's look at a losing sequence to examine how quickly our wagers can mount:

Starting Line:	1-2-3-4-5-6	+0 units
1. Bet 1 + 6, or 7 units and lose:	1-2-3-4-5-6-7	–7 units
2. Bet 1 + 7, or 8 units and lose:	1-2-3-4-5-6-7-8	–15 units
3. Bet 1 + 8, or 9 units and win:	x-2-3-4-5-6-7-x	–6 units
4. Bet 2 + 7, or 9 units and lose:	x-2-3-4-5-6-7-x-9	–15 units
5. Bet 2 + 9, or 11 units and win:	x-x-3-4-5-6-7-x-x	–4 units
6. Bet 3 + 7, or 10 units and lose:	x-x-3-4-5-6-7-x-x-10	–14 units
7. Bet 3 + 10, or 13 units and lose:	x-x-3-4-5-6-7-x-x-10-13	–27 units

—series is abandoned—

If you look at the following sequence, you will see that a couple of wins are sprinkled in for good measure, but the bettor never recovers from the first two losses. If our bettor were playing with $5 units, he would be down a whopping $135 after only three net losses (five losses minus two wins). Because there are limitless combinations of numbers to use and varying lengths of series available, it is impractical to thoroughly analyze the Labouchere. For our average loss-per-spin calculations in **Table 2-C**, I included three *ultra* conservative series of numbers: 1-2-1, 1-1 and the most conservative 1 (technically not a series). Even with a win objective of only four units per sequence (as with the 1-2-1), this system can be crippling to your bankroll. Like other systems, the more money wagered, or exposed to the house edge, the more money lost on average. Let's examine the previous sequence of wins and loses with a less aggressive starting line of 1-2-3-2-1:

Starting Line:	1-2-3-2-1	+0 units
1. Bet 1 + 1, or 2 units and lose:	1-2-3-2-1-2	–2 units
2. Bet 1 + 2, or 3 units and lose:	1-2-3-2-1-2-3	–5 units
3. Bet 1 + 3, or 4 units and win:	x-2-3-2-1-2-x	–1 unit
4. Bet 2 + 2, or 4 units and lose:	x-2-3-2-1-2-x-4	–5 units
5. Bet 2 + 4, or 6 units and win:	x-x-3-2-1-2-x-x	+1 units
6. Bet 3 + 2, or 5 units and lose:	x-x-3-2-1-2-x-x-5	–4 units
7. Bet 3 + 5, or 8 units and lose:	x-x-3-2-1-2-x-x-5-8	–12 units

—series is abandoned—

You can see that both the smaller series length and value of units used save our ill-fated bettor 15 units. At one point, the bettor actually is ahead by one unit. Here, the player sets his sights on a more modest nine unit win, so his losses are not as devastating. Please realize that a longer series of larger numbers has a remote likelihood of success. The shorter the series and smaller the values, the better the chance of winning the series. Of course, we are minimizing our exposure, and hence limiting our losses, but like all mathematical systems, the Labouchere will lose money over the long haul.

The Fibonacci

Leonardo Pisan, better known as Fibonacci, was born in Pisa (now part of Italy) in 1170 A.D. Fibonacci was a member of the Bonacci family and traveled all around the Mediterranean as a boy with his father who held a diplomatic post. His keen interest in mathematics and his exposure to other cultures allowed Fibonacci to excel in solving a wide variety of mathematical problems. Fibonacci is probably best known for discovering the Fibonacci sequence, a sequence of numbers that readily exists in nature. Although technically not a mathematical system per se, the sequence is often used in a losing or negative progression. The Fibonacci series is as follows:

1, 1, 2, 3, 5, 8, 13, 21, 34, 55, 89, 144, 233, 377, . . .

The next number in the series is simply the sum of the previous two numbers. The starting number is 1. The second number calculated from 0 + 1 (no number in front of the first 1) and is 1 again. The next number is 1 + 1 or 2, then 1 + 2 for 3, then 2 + 3 = 5 and 5 + 3 = 8, etc.

The system works similarly to the Labouchere system, only the player starts out with an empty line. If the first bet is won, then the sequence is over and the player has won. No numbers need to be written down. If the first bet is lost, then a line is started and a 1 is written down. The next number in the sequence represents the following wager size. If this bet is lost, then it is added to the end of the line. As each bet is lost, it is added to the end of the series. If a bet is won, the last number in the series is crossed out. An example here will help clarify things:

1. Bet 1 unit and lose:	1	–1 unit
2. Bet 1 unit and lose:	1-1-2–	–2 units
3. Bet 2 units and lose:	1-1-2	–4 units
4. Bet 3 units and win:	1-x-x	–1 units
5. Bet 1 unit and lose:	1-x-x-1	–2 units
6. Bet 2 units and lose:	1-x-x-1-2	–4 units
7. Bet 3 units and lose:	1-x-x-1-2-3	–7 units
8. Bet 5 units and win:	1-x-x-1-x-x	–2 units
9. Bet 2 units and lose:	1-x-x-1-x-x-2	–4 units
10. Bet 3 units and win:	1-x-x-x-x-x	–1 units
11. Bet 1 unit and lose:	1-x-x-x-x-x-1	–2 units
12. Bet 2 units and win:	x-x-x-x-x-x-x	+0 units
13. Bet 1 unit and win:	stop	+1 unit

—series has been won—

Our player starts off with a one-unit loss, so a 1 is recorded to start the line. Another 1 is added after the second wager of one unit loses. The third stake requires a two-unit wager and loses, so a 2 is added. The fourth bet of three units finally wins and the 1-2 can be cancelled from the line. Because each wager adds up to the previous two bets, the last two numbers on the line can be crossed out when a bet wins. The next three bets lose, escalating our eighth stake up to five units. Our player experiences a win at this level, allowing him to cancel out the 2-3 at the end of the line. The ninth bet of two units loses, so the line grows to 1-1-2. A win, loss and win on the tenth, eleventh and twelfth wagers finally wipe out the betting line. The player needs and gets a win at this point to go up a net profit of one unit and win the sequence.

With only five wins and eight losses, this particular sequence of wins and losses is tough, but our player is able to pull it out. On the eighth wager, the stake reaches a high of five units. If that bet would have lost, our player would be twelve units in the hole. At a $5 unit size, that equates to a $60 deficit. The next wager from here would be eight units and another loss would put him back 20 units total. If you elect to use the Fibonacci, I would highly recommend that you limit your top bet to five units. If you lose your wager at this level, then abandon the series. Things get ugly too quickly from here. Stop and regroup. Let's take the Fibonacci up to twelve straight losses to see how quickly the wagers can mount:

1. Bet 1 unit and lose:	1	–1 units
2. Bet 1 unit and lose:	1-1	–2 units
3. Bet 2 units and lose:	1-1-2	–4 units
4. Bet 3 units and lose:	1-1-2-3	–7 units
5. Bet 5 units and lose:	1-1-2-3-5	–12 units
6. Bet 8 units and lose:	1-1-2-3-5-8	–20 units
7. Bet 13 units and lose:	1-1-2-3-5-8-13	–33 units
8. Bet 21 units and lose:	1-1-2-3-5-8-13-21	–54 units
9. Bet 34 units and lose:	1-1-2-3-5-8-13-21-34	–88 units
10. Bet 55 units and lose:	1-1-2-3-5-8-13-21-34-55	–143 units
11. Bet 89 units and lose:	1-1-2-3-5-8-13-21-34-55-89	–232 units
12. Bet 144 units and lose:	1-1-2-3-5-8-13-21-34-55-89-144	–376 units

This last example demonstrates how the bets can mount in a string of twelve losses. The chances of losing twelve straight on a double zero roulette wheel are $(20/38)^{12}$ = 0.0004518, or about one shot in 2213. The purpose here was to show a range of cumulative losses and let the system player decide where to draw the line. Some authors show the Fibonacci sequence and omit the first 1 in the series. That's fine, but the shortened version is a little more aggressive than the full Fibonacci. You will lose a bit more money on average with this abbreviated variation. All in all, the Fibonacci sequence doesn't fare to badly. This system can be fun and not too damaging if you limit your top bet to five units.

Oscar's Grind

The first reference I can find regarding this more modern betting system appeared in Allan Wilson's *The Casino Gambler's Guide*, copyright 1965. Wilson was intrigued with this system after a dice player named "Oscar" produced detailed records showing modest, but consistent profits. Wilson ran 280,000 sequence simulations on an IBM 790 mainframe computer that was available to him. The analysis showed that while Oscar was a bit on the luckier side, his claims were at least possible. Now remember that Oscar was a pass line bettor only attempting to buck a –1.414% house edge as compared to a –5.263% house edge for double-zero roulette. In addition, Oscar had a mega-bankroll and the willingness to risk it all for a one unit per cycle win.

Let's look at the details of the Grind. The system has the player bet one unit. If he wins, the sequence is over and a new one can be initiated. If the wager is lost, then the next bet will be the same size as the one just lost. Whenever a bet is won, the next stake is one unit larger, unless it causes the bettor to net more than one unit of profit for the sequence. At that point, just enough is wagered to net one unit if the bet wins. That's it! A sample sequence might look like this:

1.	Bet 1 unit and lose:	−1 unit
2.	Bet 1 unit and win:	+0 units
3.	Bet 1 unit and lose:	−1 unit
4.	Bet 1 unit and lose:	−2 units
5.	Bet 1 unit and lose:	−3 units
6.	Bet 1 unit and win:	−2 units
7.	Bet 2 units and win:	+0 units
8.	Bet 1 unit and lose:	−1 unit
9.	Bet 1 unit and win:	+0 units
10.	Bet 1 unit and win:	+1 unit

—series has been won—

The player starts off with a loss so his second stake remains at one unit. This bet is won, putting him back to even. Because he is only seeking a one-unit win for the progression, he does not escalate his bet to two units. Bets 3 through 5 are losers so he stays with a one-unit stake. After the sixth bet wins, he increases his wager to two units. The seventh bet also wins, but again he only needs a one unit bet to win the sequence. The eighth bet loses so the ninth wager is one unit. Finally, the tenth bet wins and our player wins the entire progression. Notice that out of ten total wagers, nine were only one unit in size. This system tends to be more conservative and less volatile. The sequence illustrated above contained five wins and five losses. I like the fact that this system does not quickly escalate your losing wagers and blindside you like some of the others. However, as your losses outnumber your wins, the amount you must wager after a win will steadily mount. Take a look at the following *tree diagram* to see all the possibilities for a progression up to five bets deep:

Like the other mathematical systems, this staking system will lose over a sustained period. They all have their Achilles heel. The Grind seems to stall in choppy games. You increase your stake after a win and then lose the larger wager, so you lower your next bet but you win that one. This back-and-forth-type sequence can add losses up quickly. Where Oscar's Grind really works well is in streaky games. The Grind minimizes your betting level if you are amidst a string

Oscar's Grind Tree Diagram
(5-bet progression using a $5 unit)

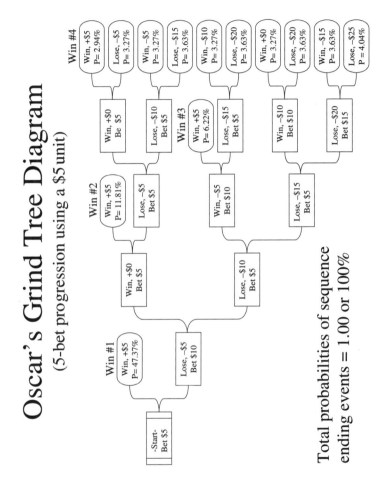

Total probabilities of sequence
ending events = 1.00 or 100%

Diagram 2-B
Oscar's Grind Tree Diagram

of losses. It also directs you to gradually increase your wagers during a streak of wins, helping to optimize profits. This can be one of the safer systems to use if you limit your maximum bet or impose a stop-loss parameter for choppy games. Look at **Table 2-C** to check how well this system stacks up on average against the others. If you plan on using Oscar's Grind, I would recommend a stop-loss of about ten, no more than 12 units per cycle.

The Cuban

Another modern system originated in Cuba before Fidel Castro took control. It is more appropriately called the Cuban, but sometimes referred to as the black third column system. This system has the player make a one-unit wager on the third column (which pays 2 to 1) and another one on the even-money black numbers. Supposedly, the player has a free chance at scalping off one unit of profit per spin. The logic behind this system reasons that there are only four black numbers in the third column leaving eight red ones. Because you are covering so many red numbers, you will place an insurance bet on black. If a red third column number appears then you win one unit. If a non–third column number hits, then the chances of it being black are greater. Because you have a wager on black, your black bet will win back the unit that you lost on the third column, breaking you even. If you hit a non–third column red number and lose both bets, this is supposed to be offset by the possibility of hitting a black third column number, winning both wagers. Hence, it would appear that you have one way to lose two units which is balanced with one way to win two units, one way to break-even and then one way to net one unit. Wow! This is great. Finally a mathematical system that works! . . . or not. Let's take a closer look at this one. For convenience, we will look at one cycle of 38 spins and calculate the average win (or loss). As we stated earlier, there are four possibilities, but we must also consider their frequency of occurrence for a correct assessment:

1. A black, third column number results and the player nets one unit on black and two units on the third column. There are four black third column numbers so this will occur four times out of 38 trials.

2. A red, third column number appears. The player will win two units on the third column, but lose one unit on the black wager, netting one unit total. This will happen eight times in 38 spins on average.

3. A black, non–third column number hits. The player will win one unit on black but lose one unit on the third column wager, thus, breaking even. There are 14 ways to break even.

4. A non-black, non–third column number results (remember that there are two green zeroes). The player will lose both bets, or two units. There are ten red, non–third column numbers plus two zeroes. That's twelve ways out of 38 to lose both bets.

Let us complete our calculation:

1. 4 times our player will win 3 units: 4 x 3 units   = +12 units

2. 8 times our bettor will win 1 unit: 8 x 1 unit   = +8 units

3. 14 times our bettor will break-even: 14 x 0 units = +0 units

4. 12 times our player will lose two units: 12 x 2 units = –24 units

38 total times   **= –4 units**

Two units per spin with 38 spins equals 76 total units wagered. This system will lose four units out of 76 on average over 38 spins (–4 units/76 units wagered = –5.263%, a negative player's edge). If this system were played on a single zero wheel, then only 22 units would be lost while 20 units are won (–2 units/76 units wagered = –2.703% edge). Throw in a half unit if surrender is possible and you have -1.5 units/76 units wagered = –1.974% average edge. One feature that I like about this system is that the player is not necessarily called upon to increase his wager after a loss or win. He can wager the same two units each time. This is a flat betting system that will not kill the system player, but it will lose money over an extended period of time.

Flat Betting

Speaking of the flat bet, another system, although technically there is no progression of bets, is something I refer to as the flat betting system. A flat bet is a bet that does not increase or decrease with losses or wins. It simply stays *flat* or fixed in its amount. The flat betting system will lose the least amount of money (see **Table 2-C**) when starting with the same unit size as the other systems. You can operate this system just like any other mathematically-based system. Simply bet one unit on any even-money wager that you desire. If you win that bet, the sequence is won and you stop to claim a one-unit victory. If you lose that bet, then continue to wager one unit until your wins outnumber your losses by one. At this point, you will have one unit net profit and will win the sequence. You can either quit betting or begin a new cycle. Because you are flat betting, the length of your sequence does not hurt nearly as bad as it would for a progressive system. To win the sequence, your total wins must be one more than your total losses. This system may seem boring to implement, but it is the safest of all.

Calculated Losses for Each System

The average losses for each system described were calculated and recorded below in **Table 2-C**. A betting progression of up to five bets deep was used as the common cutoff point. Because the Labouchere can be applied to *any* series of numbers that the player chooses to use, there are infinite possibilities to consider. I have included three different series that help define a playable range of conservative Laboucheres. Anything more than the 1-2-1 series is not reasonable for roulette. Calculations for each system are based on a $5 unit size. If you wish to know what your average loss per cycle would be for, say a Fibonacci using a $25 unit size, just multiply –99 cents times five (which is $25/$5) to get –$4.95/cycle. Your average loss per spin would similarly be –35.3 cents times five, or –177 cents per spin. Most authors tell you that mathematical systems will lose you money and leave it at that. While this is true, I know that some of you will persist in using them. Referring to the data in **Table 2-C**, you will at least know what you are up against.

Table 2-C System Loss Averages (5-bet progression, $5 unit)				
Mathematical System	Average Spins/Cycle	Average Loss/Cycle	Average Loss/Spin	System Ranking
Martingale	2.026	$1.46	72.3 cents	7th
Grand Martingale	2.026	$2.40	118.2 cents	9th
D'Alembert	2.295	$1.19	51.9 cents	5th
Labouchere, 1-2-1	3.460	$5.60	161.7 cents	10th (worst)
Labouchere, 1-1	2.495	$1.99	79.8 cents	8th
Labouchere, 1	2.295	$1.14	49.5 cents	4th
Fibonacci	2.807	$0.99	35.3 cents	3rd
Oscar's Grind	2.807	$0.79	28.3 cents	2nd
Cuban	1.000	$0.53	52.6 cents	6th
Flat Bet	2.869	$0.76	26.4 cents	1st (safest)

The Probability of a Run

Let's say that the casino you frequent the most has six roulette tables. On each of these tables you will find three sets of even-money wagers: red versus black, odd versus even and high versus low. That presents 18 possible runs at any given time. The chances of any one of these groups having a losing run of, say, six in a row is $(20/38)6$, or 0.02126. That's about one chance in 47. Now factor in three such sets at each table times six tables and your chances of encountering such

a run are 18/47. That works out to be 38+% of the time! A run
of say, six blacks, or any even-money group of numbers, isn't
as rare as you might think! How about a run of eight losses in
a casino with 12 roulette tables? When multiplied by 36,
(20/38)8, or 0.00589 gives us 0.21197, a better than 21% chance
of finding a run of eight. These events will happen, and when
they do, think back and remember what you read here.
Imagine if you had been doubling up against one of these
monsters from the get-go!!

Final Thoughts on Mathematical Systems

Obviously, the less we play, the less we lose. Some
methods are worse than others. My recommendations, if you
must play a mathematical system, are as follows:

1. Wait for a particular group to be absent for six to eight
    spins before running a progression on it. Do not start
    betting right away. If there are four or less wheels open,
    then wait for a string of six losses (or absences) before
    you place your first wager. If there are five to ten
    wheels in play, then seven losses will suffice. Anything
    over ten wheels will require a losing run of eight. If
    your casino has more than ten active tables, you may
    choose to pick just five or six tables to watch.
    Technically speaking, waiting for a string of losses
    before betting will not increase your chances of win-
    ning, but it will keep you off the tables more (minimiz-
    ing exposure and losses).

2. Stay away from the Labouchere (cancellation) or
    Martingale (double up) systems. They will lose you the
    most money. If you must use the Martingale system,
    run a progression only two or three bets deep at the
    most. Avoid the Grand Martingale. Oscar's Grind with
    a stop-loss of ten units or flat betting is the safest way

to system stake. The Fibonacci is not bad with a cap of five units for the top bet.

3. Determine how many units you will reasonably be satisfied with winning for your session. If you reach your goal, consider yourself lucky and cash in. By the same token, select a stop-loss point and stick with it. If you begin to win, then adjust your stop-loss to follow your highest balance. That way you will never lose more than ten units off your peak. This is known as a trailing stop-loss. If you like, you can tighten, or make your trailing stop-loss smaller after each win to help ensure a winning session.

4. If you can find a lower stakes single-zero wheel to wager on, or a wheel offering surrender on even money wagers, then your bankroll will last longer. Do not play a single-zero wheel with $25 minimums over a double-zero wheel with $5 minimums unless you are a high-spender. Err . . . I mean—roller! Even with flat betting, 2.703% of $25 (almost 68 cents per wager) is a greater tax to pay than 5.263% of $5 (about 26 cents per bet).

5. Don't bet with your emotions! If you lose a few units . . . fine. Take a walk and clear your head. *Never go chasing a falling piano!*

If you play a mathematical system, please stick to the above guidelines. They will cut your losses dramatically. Realize that system playing is for entertainment. You are limiting your losses while occasionally getting lucky. Refer to the data in **Table 2-C**. Please, do not get duped into thinking that you have purchased or stumbled upon some secret, unique money-making system just because it is not listed above. They will all prove to be losers if given ample opportunity. I am not saying that all mathematically-based betting systems are terrible, although some are much worse than others. I am merely stating that in a game of independent trials, you cannot win over the long haul by simply manipulating bets. Certain systems are entertaining and may help with money management. Most betting systems do have *some* accounting and organizational benefits. Just do not believe that your system will magically produce all the easy money that an able-bodied player is capable of carrying out of the casino!

Of course, being totally disorganized and having no idea where you stand financially, is probably worse. I have seen people with absolutely no money management system at all. I am sure that you've seen them, too. These people might play $400 or $500 worth of nickels ($5 chips) on a variety of numbers, in a variety of bet types, and in varying amounts. I call these players sprinklers. They rely purely on luck and the casinos L-O-V-E these guys. They'll put two chips straight up on number 4, five chips on the 12-15 split, a single chip on some corner bet, four straight up on the double zero . . . you get the picture. They will cover most of the 38 possible numbers in one way or another as the mood strikes them.

Sprinklers never seem to know how much money they have out on the layout. They will hit a number with $10 straight up and break out into a celebration dance, not realizing that $425 worth of bets was lost to win that $350. How can they? There is no practical accounting system that can track all of the numerous combinations of bet types and wage sizes that they can concoct. All of the sprinklers I've witnessed simply play until they run out of chips. After they exhaust all of their funds, they then have to make a *conscious* decision to leave or visit the ATM machines conveniently located nearby. There is no plan or fixed goal in mind. At least most systems that I've seen determine betting size, follow some sort of pattern and have some kind of objective to shoot for. Money management is a critical tool for the advantage player, but it alone cannot guarantee success, only gauge it.

If hunches, favorites or betting systems will not work over the long haul, what's left? It occurred to me that there was another side to the problem . . . the physical mechanics of a single roulette spin. You must understand the physical phenomena involved in a single roulette trial and use telltale signs to predict the sector most likely to capture the ball. You need to play the wheel head, not the betting layout. If your *predictive* method garners you a positive edge over the house, then flat betting is all the mathematical system you will ever need!

What It Takes to Rule over Roulette

We now know that we must understand the physical elements at play in a single roulette trial. We will take a closer look here and in the following section to study the mechanics involved. In subsequent sections we will learn how to analyze the mechanical conditions of a particular roulette spin and use telltale signs to predict which sector will most likely to capture the ball. We will learn to play the *wheel head*, not the betting baize! Let us look at what happens in any given trial.

A Single Spin of the Wheel

In North America, the wheel head is usually spun in a counterclockwise direction while the ball is launched clockwise. The rotor, or wheel head, (I use both interchangeably) is a heavy disk weighing as much as 25 lbs. Because of its mass and shape, it has a large mass moment of inertia. The rotor is—and acts—just like a flywheel. Once it is spinning, the rotor will tend to continue doing so with just a minimal kick administered periodically by the dealer. In addition, the rotor is balanced atop a central spindle and usually is mounted between dual precision bearing assemblies, one at its base, and the other just under the turret. This goes a long way towards removing most elements of friction on the rotor. These two factors explain why a properly maintained rotor with a solid initial thrust will spin for up to ten minutes before coming to a complete stop. Thus, for the life of a single roulette trial, some 10 to 15 seconds, the wheel head is considered to have negligible decay in its angular velocity. Therefore, over the brief life of a *single roulette spin*, the wheel head is considered to rotate at a constant speed.

The dealer, or croupier snaps the ball in the opposite direction of the spinning rotor. It orbits around the upper track in a horizontal circle until the acceleration due to gravity overcomes the centrifugal acceleration. The centrifugal acceleration provides the force needed to hold the ball in the upper track. This acceleration (or deceleration) exponentially decays due to several ball factors. The ball, probably being made of nylon or acetate, weighs only a few ounces and experiences much entropic degradation. Because of its light weight, the ball is quickly slowed by the effects of rolling friction, wind resistance and gravity. Once the ball leaves the upper track, it is nothing more than a short spiral down the conical apron towards the spinning rotor. This apron is laden with eight elongated ball deflectors, evenly spaced and alternately oriented vertically then horizontally. The vertical deflectors or diamonds tend to direct the ball more quickly onto the rotor, while the horizontal deflectors tend to extend the ball's trajectory, causing it to enter the rotor more tangentially. These deflectors do not always change or affect the ball's path. In fact, sometimes they are missed altogether. Still, they are ever present and can present a difficulty in determining where the ball will eventually end up.

Many times the ball experiences a spattering effect when contacting the pocket separators, otherwise known as frets, on the moving wheel head. The ball may stay in the initial strike pocket, bounce forward some number of pockets (typical), impact the fret head-on and bounce backward (same direction of wheel), or it may pop up landing in any number of different places. The ball may also get suspended on the cone area or shot back up on the apron, or even out of the roulette wheel altogether! A rapidly spinning rotor causes the ball's reaction to be much more volatile and hence more unpredictable.

Now that we have a good idea of what transpires during a single roulette trial, we are in a better position to understand the advantage systems and how professional players use them. There are two expert level systems that take advantage of the physical phenomena involved under different circumstances. We will take a detailed look at those in **Section 4**.

The first professional level method that we will discuss requires countless hours of scouting, some initial analysis, and repeatedly betting on the same number(s). It seeks out and exploits wheels that are *biased*, or tend to favor a particular number or group of numbers. The second pro system, *wheel tracking* sometimes called *wheel watching* or *visual tracking*, requires much study and practice, some scouting, and the ability to perform split second analyses and immediate bet placements. There are perhaps a dozen people worldwide that are capable of competently employing this second system.

In **Section 5**, we will discuss advantage systems for the serious part-time player to use. These last advantage systems involve something referred to as *dealer's signature* or *dealer's bias* approaches. They are based on the same principles used in wheel tracking and computer prediction methods. The traditional dealer's signature method is a much–watered down, physically predictive approach. It assumes that the mechanical conditions needed for predictive play, remain constant from trial to trial. You simply study the numbers that come up and look for patterns. These patterns tell you which rotor sector to play next. As a result, there are fewer calculations and a lot less understanding needed to execute this method. The tradeoff, however is that the dealer's signature method is not quite as reliable. We will discuss a hybrid approach that reasonably balances the tradeoffs, but first we will get more intimate with the workings of a roulette wheel in **Section 3**.

Part 3

Roulette Wheel:

Construction and Layout

The roulette wheels of today are high-tech, precision cast, machined and assembled to exacting tolerances. Through the deployment of computer-aided design and analysis, the wheel has been optimized for longer life and better performance. Computer numerical-controlled machining processes and space-age bearing assemblies, composites, wood laminates and other materials all help to create an attractive yet durable, high-quality wheel. Although different manufacturers will have slightly different features, all roulette wheels contain two main subassemblies: the stationery housing or bowl, and the rotating wheel head, sometimes called the rotor or cylinder. **Diagram 3-A** shows the basic components that make up a typical roulette wheel.

The outer bowl is 32 inches in diameter and provides a stationery housing for the gaming device. It is made up of solid wood, wood composite with finished wood veneer or plastic laminate or high-impact plastic with laminate. The bowl assembly contains the outer rim, the upper ball track (around which the ball is initially spun) and the apron, or lower ball track. Eight (sometimes 16) equally spaced canoes, or ball deflectors are mounted around the apron to alter the ball's final approach. They are alternately positioned, horizontally then vertically. The horizontal deflectors tend to extend the ball's path, creating a more shallow, grazing angle of entry. The vertical deflectors, on the other hand, tend to shorten the ball's entry. When the ball strikes a vertical deflector, it usually takes a right-hand turn directly onto the num-

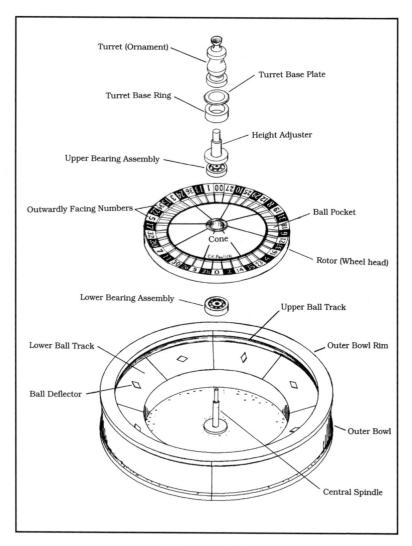

Diagram 3-A
Roulette Wheel Construction

bered rotor. The bowl also contains a central, vertically orientated shaft or spindle. At the base of this central spindle is a tightly fitted, lower-bearing assembly about which the rotor or wheel head is positioned.

The rotor is about 20 inches in diameter and fits over the top lower bearing assembly and spindle. Because of its mass and shape, this heavy, cylindrical disk processes a large mass moment of inertia. The inertial properties and low friction bearings create a flywheel effect, allowing the wheel head to spin at a constant speed (or angular velocity) for a surprisingly long period of time. The outer circumference of the wheel head contains a series of 37 or 38 outwardly facing numbers that align and correspond to a concentric ring of 37 or 38 pockets just inside the numbers. These pockets are separated by pocket separators, or frets. Some manufacturers make a solid, one-piece fret ring that can be rotated with respect to the numbered rotor. Other manufacturers cast and affix individual frets between each pocket. Inside the ring of pockets is the cone. If the ball should stray inside the ring of pockets, the incline of the cone will direct it back towards the pockets.

Inside the top of the rotor and around the central spindle is the top bearing assembly. Most rotors will employ two main bearing assemblies. Over the top of the upper-bearing assembly is a mechanism for adjusting the rotor height. It is important that the rotor height is flush with the apron where the ball makes its final approach. If the rotor is too low, then the ball will take a dead drop right into one of the pockets with little bounce. If the rotor is situated too high, then the ball will be marooned at the outer edge of the rotor, unable to climb on board and drop into one of the pockets.

The turret base ring is a decorative metal collar that fits over the height adjuster's base and upper bearing assembly. It is a component that sits atop the rotor's cone. Capping off the turret base ring is a round, finished piece called the turret-base plate. Concealing the height adjuster and perched on top of the turret-base plate is the turret itself. This is a very decorative piece, sometimes referred to as the ornament. On the underside of this entire rigid, rather heavy gaming device (weighing upwards of 100 pounds) is a set of three or four leveling feet. A wheel that is sufficiently tilted will make roulette prediction easier because the ball is more likely to exit the upper track while laboring to get up to the apex of the tilt. Knowing where the ball will exit the upper ball track eliminates one of the main variables from the prediction equation. Casinos often do not take the time to level their wheels properly and this can be taken advantage of by astute players.

The Roulette Ball

The roulette ball is a precision molded spheroid. According to New Jersey law, the roulette ball shall be made completely of a nonmetallic substance and not be *less* than 3/4 of an inch nor *more* than 7/8 of an inch in diameter, unless otherwise approved by the commission. This seems to be about the typical size employed everywhere. European manufacturers make an 18 mm (slightly less than 3/4 of an inch) and a 21 mm (a little smaller than 7/8 of an inch) diameter balls. The ball is spun in the opposite direction of the wheel head and must complete at least four full revolutions around the upper track of the wheel to constitute a valid spin. The size and weight of the roulette ball will have a definite effect on the outcome. A larger, heavier ball will plunk down into the nearest pocket with little reaction. A smaller, lighter ball will bounce all over the wheel head, and perhaps out of the wheel entirely. Also, a lighter ball may get hung up on the central cone where wind resistance and the centrifugal force offset the effects of gravity. When this happens, the ball cannot settle into a pocket and a "no spin" is called. Because the smaller roulette balls are too lively and the larger balls tend to die too quickly, casinos usually employ a mid-sized ball of 13/16 inches in diameter.

In addition to the ball's size and shape, its material will affect its weight and elastic properties. A roulette ball with a higher coefficient of restitution will produce a more lively reaction when contacting deflectors and pocket separators. Teflon is a heavier material and will deaden quicker. Composition balls (like those used for billiards) are a little lighter than Teflon, but still a bit on the heavy side. Ivory is right in the middle, however, its use is prohibited in most areas. Acetal, a common substance for roulette balls, is a lighter to mid-range material with a decent amount of ball action. This is a happy medium for the casinos. Nylon is too light and highly volatile. If it meets up with a swiftly rotating wheel head, you may not be able to keep the ball inside the wheel. Another effect that the material can have on the ball's performance is the amount of spin imparted. Just as the Earth spins about its own axis while simultaneously orbiting the sun, a roulette ball will do likewise. As it circles the upper ball track of the outer rim, it will also spin about its own axis. The amount of spin that the ball experiences is tied to the specific gravity of the material used. Every material has a specific gravity, which is a measure of its weight-per-unit volume. A ball produced from a lower specific gravity material will exhibit faster rotation about its own axis. This spin energy must be completely exhausted before the ball can come to rest in one of the pockets. Hence, the more spin energy the ball possesses, the greater the reaction as the ball contacts the pocket separators.

The Upper Ball Track

The more modern wheel designs employ a new type of upper ball track. Previously, the upper ball tracks had a ledge, or slight lip, that helped hold the ball in the track right up to the point where the acceleration due to gravity was distinctly greater than the centrifugal acceleration. Once the ball dropped off the ledge, it was no more than a short spiral down to the wheel head. By removing the ledge in the upper ball track, the ball is influenced more heavily by *both* accelerations at the same time. As the centrifugal acceleration gradually diminishes, the acceleration due to gravity can now pull the ball slowly out of the upper track. There is no line of demarcation, so the ball experiences a gradual escape from the outer rim. Its approach down the apron, or lower ball track, is longer and more gradual as well. If the ball now covers *half* the apron when approaching the rotor instead of just a quarter, then it is *twice* as likely to contact one of the deflectors which will alter its path. The more distance the ball travels in the lower ball track, the greater the chance for error using a physical prediction or tracking method. In addition, the more shallow angle makes it more difficult to judge exactly where the ball will cross over onto the rotor.

If a wheel has a warped or otherwise non-round upper ball track, the ball will not have an equal chance to exit the track at any point. This defect can occur during the manufacturing process or over years of usage. When a dealer launches the roulette ball, he is pressing it up against the ball track just before he snaps the ball. The dealer will routinely snap the ball from the same point in the track every time. The pressure from snapping the ball causes uneven wear in one area of the track and if the wheel isn't rotated 10 or 15 degrees on a regular basis, then this wear will affect the point of ball drop. Any anomaly in the track can cause a consistent drop point.

An obstruction or irregularity in the track can cause the ball to eject much earlier than nature would dictate. The upper track is assembled from sections, and at the juncture of any two sections is a seam. An uneven track seam will create a step or obstruction to the ball. Even something as seemingly minor as a little excess lacquer on a given spot in the track will affect the ball's departure. Anything that causes the ball to exit the upper track at some consistent point favors the observant player, while a more random upper-track exit enforces the casino's mathematical edge. In **Part 4**, I will discuss how to generate octant drop histograms and how to use them for our benefit.

The Ball Deflectors

Ball deflectors are designed to alter the ball's path in the lower ball track or apron. They are usually made of stainless steel and look like upside down canoes or diamonds. There are eight of these evenly spaced deflectors that alternate orientations, first horizontally, then vertically. The canoe- or elliptical-shaped deflectors are the more traditional style. They actually look like capsized canoes drifting around the lower bowl. Then there are those that appear to be elongated pyramids with four distinctive flat, triangular surfaces. These deflectors tend to have a more varied effect on the ball.

I've seen ball deflectors that look like two opposing cones welded base-to-base and mounted in the lower bowl. These have more of a deadening effect on the ball. Another popular deflector style is the flat diamond. This deflector is a diamond shape and steps up slightly where it is flat across the top. The ball is impeded slightly or deflected slightly—or both. There may be other styles of ball deflectors around that I have not run across as I have not played in every casino in the world. If you plan on becoming a serious predictive player, you will want to note the type of ball deflector and what effects it has on the ball—and on your game.

While the use of ball deflectors seems to introduce yet another set of random variables into the predictive player's equation, sometimes the right combination of elements can work in your favor. I found that a sufficiently tilted wheel *whose apex occurs just before a vertical deflector* may create an advantage for the astute player. Not only does the player know where the ball will drop from, but he will also have a deflector there to funnel the ball right onto the rotor. The ball's forward momentum is partially or wholly negated by colliding with the vertical deflector. Once the ball has been "tamed" by the more massive deflector, it will drop quickly onto the rotor. Without even a struggle, the ball will die quietly in one of the nearby pockets.

I ran into this situation at the Stardust Hotel on my last trip to Vegas. There were three roulette tables set up on the end of a blackjack pit. The wheels were older, higher-profile models with *deep* pockets. The busy dealer was maintaining a consistent clockwork rhythm to the game—spin the ball, collect the losers, pay the winners. The ball was breaking just to the left of the dealer and hitting a vertical deflector. It made an immediate right-hand turn onto the rotor and remained in the first pocket that it encountered. I bought in for fifty $1 chips and simultaneously played and tracked the ball drop. The ball broke almost 50 percent of the time from the same octant and struck the same deflector with close to 40 percent regularity! My $1 chips soon turned into $5 chips. Then I began stacking $5 chips. By the time I colored my chips up to $25 values, a concerned boss was on the phone and two "suits" were watching me. My first wager at the $25 unit level yielded me a straight up hit on the number 2 . . . 875 big ones! One of the bosses walked over and asked if I had a casino-rating card. I answered "no," and decided to cash out at that point. If you find a wheel like this in a casino that you visit on a regular basis, you may want to milk it slowly, but, if not, give me a call!

The Pocket Separators

On either side of every pocket is a radially oriented separator or fret. These separators are what slow down and eventually hold the ball in a particular pocket. They are made of a nonferrous metal and usually plated with chrome or brass. The older-style roulette wheels have individual frets with a higher profile. The pockets are deep and the fret walls are high, so the ball does not jump around too much after it contacts the rotor. This is a predictive player's dream. If he can tell where the ball will cross over onto the rotor, then he knows it won't bounce more than two or three pockets away.

It is important from the casinos' and manufacturers' stand points that each fret is identical in shape and size. Depending on the casting or stamping method and the way the frets are plated, the tolerances may widely vary. If frets are individually made and fixed to the rotor, it is important that the manufacturer measure the thickness, height and length of each pocket separator. Separators should be closely grouped with other frets of the same shape and dimensions. If the variance in shape or size is too great, then the differing frets will cause a bias that favors certain pockets.

If one fret is lower in height than the others, it will more easily permit the ball to skip over it. The pocket in front of the lower fret has a lessened chance of capturing the ball. Conversely, a higher fret is more likely to capture the ball and as such, the pocket directly in front of it will see more than its fair share of action. If a fret or pocket separator is thicker than normal, it will cause one or both of the adjacent pockets to be smaller in width. The smaller the pocket, the less the chance of containing the ball. Likewise, a thinner than normal pocket fret will create a wider pocket with a greater opportunity for catching the ball. The length of a fret may have an effect on where the ball ends up. A fret that is longer than the others has a better chance of not allowing the ball to roll around it, while a shorter fret will more likely allow a ball to pass. Individual pocket separators are usually riveted or fixed with tiny screws. After years of use, the fasteners get loose and so do the frets. A loose fret will vibrate when struck, absorbing some or all of the ball's energy. If the ball's kinetic energy is used up, the ball will come to rest.

As you can see, any separator irregularity can potentially create a *pocket bias*. The strength of the bias will depend on the deviance from the norm. The more irregular the fret, the stronger the bias. Also, a group of slightly irregular frets with the same abnormalities that are adjacent to each other may create a *biased sector*. For example, a group of five slightly higher frets that are all positioned in the same area, or sector of the wheel, will have a greater chance of stopping the ball within this region of the rotor. This would be a bias-player's dream. It is not necessarily important that you know why a wheel is biased as much as what pocket or pockets are biased. Later, we will show you how to use statistics to verify a pocket or sector bias. As wheel manufacturers began to realize that savvy players were cashing in on the contained-ball movement of the traditionally higher fret models, and the potential biases caused by using individual frets, they created lower-profile wheels. These wheels allowed more ball bounce and required less service. The new lower profile separators were half as high as their predecessor's were.

Any material object will possess a point about which all its weight can be balanced. This point is the center of gravity. A homogeneous-materialed roulette ball will have its center of gravity exactly at the ball's center. If the ball is 3/4 inches in diameter, then the effective weight center, or center of gravity, is half that, or 3/8 inches up from the contact point of the supporting surface. If a pocket separator's height is less than 3/8 inches, then the ball's forward momentum will more easily propel it over the pocket wall. This makes for a livelier game. The more bounce that the ball experiences, the more random (and less predictable) the outcome. Along with the lower fret designs come shallower pockets and a lower inclined cone.

The term *low-profile wheel* is used to describe this collection of features. These low profile separators may be individual pieces or a continuous ring that is machined from one solid piece of high-quality aluminum or brass. The continuous rings can be rotated or repositioned with respect to the rotor. This helps to thwart attacks by bias-wheel players.

Another more recent innovation that follows along the same lines, is the continuous-fret or scalloped-pocket design. A removable and rotatable, continuous fret is concentrically positioned just inside the ring of numbers. This separator ring contains 37 or 38 evenly spaced conical-like depressions that radiate outward from the cone. As the ball enters the rotor and contacts these depressions, it is gradually slowed and will come to rest in one of them. Because the pocket depth of these scallops varies from the cone to the numbered ring, the extent of the ball collision will vary as it contacts each pocket. I've seen the ball cross onto a slowly moving rotor, hit the deepest part of the scallop right away and bounce only three or four pockets down before stopping. Then there are the times when the rotor is spinning a little faster and the ball never gets an opportunity to contact the bottoms of the pockets until much later. The ball just merrily hop-scotches its way around the entire wheel head before coming to rest. With this type of pocket design, the effects of wheel speed, the size and material of the roulette ball and where the ball strikes each pocket will create a greater spectrum of possible reactions.

Some of the Major Manufacturers

Some of the old American masters like Benteler, Rude and B.C. Wills have yielded operations or retired from the business. Paul Tramble, a wheel maker in Reno, Nevada, had a solid reputation for high quality and fine craftsmanship. Tramble produced attractive wheels with many wood laminates and individual pocket frets that were, what I would call,

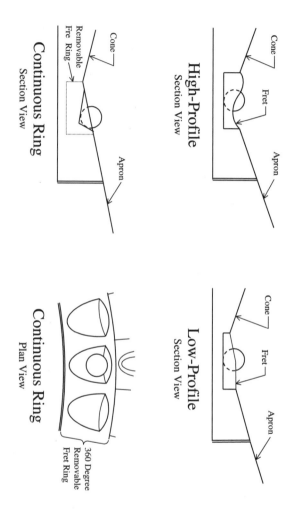

Diagram 3-B
High, Low and Continuous Frets

medium profile, as they limited ball spatter to a manageable affair for the predictive player. Because of the older bearing design and individual pocket separators, this wheel could form a bias if poorly maintained or serviced. Tramble retired in 1996 and sold his operation to the Bud Jones Company in Las Vegas, Nevada.

Bud Jones continued to create roulette wheels with the same eye for quality. The Bud Jones Company is not new to the gaming industry. They were founded in 1965 by the man whose name the company bears. I spoke with an account executive at Bud Jones who informed me that they were recently sold to Bourgoune Et Grasset, a French company that manufactures casino chips. He did not know what the future held in store for the Bud Jones roulette wheel. I guess we will have to just wait and see.

Another big American name in the wheel manufacturing business is Paulson Gaming Supplies, Inc. They are the largest gaming-equipment manufacturer for the casino industry with over 50 years of experience. With offices throughout North America, their main corporate office is in Las Vegas, Nevada. Paulson has a reputation for cutting-edge innovation, introducing new compounds and technologies to the art of wheel making. Their Modular model wheel employs non-ferrous metals such as solid brass, stress-relieved aluminum and stainless steel to prevent any magnetization in their wheels. The separator ring, machined from solid brass, was designed with a lower separator height. The one-piece pocket separator ring eliminates the chance of separators working loose and can be routinely rotated with respect to the rest of the numbered rotor. This virtually eliminates the possibility of a pocket bias from forming. The entire outer bowl and ball track is tooled from one solid block of ebonite, the same material used in bowling balls. This reduces maintenance and helps ensure against irregularities in the upper ball track.

The outside of the wheel is clad with wood laminate. Although this wheel has certain safeguards against forming biases, it has some redeeming qualities for the predictive roulette player. Ball deflectors, shaped more like diamonds than canoes, are smaller and flatter than average, having less of an effect on the ball's final trajectory as it spirals toward the rotor. In addition, the ball action is moderate (and more predictable) once the ball enters the rotor.

Across the pond in London, England, we find another quality manufacturer with over 50 years of experience in the industry. John Huxley began by producing hand-crafted gaming tables and roulette wheels. Later, Huxley grew to offer other products for the gaming industry. After the Gaming Act was passed in the United Kingdom and gambling began to flourish on almost every continent, the company successfully grew with the new and emerging markets. Huxley has developed a reputation for quality and innovation. Their research and development program designed and produced the first winning number display. They're also responsible for producing the Mark series of roulette wheels, containing the first low-profile wheel and fret design. The fret, or pocket separator, has a low knife-edged top, inducing ball bounce and promoting overall action. As if this weren't enough, they more recently developed a new continuous-fret model called the Starburst. This wheel has one continuous, and movable, fret ring with 37 or 38 conical depressions evenly spaced around it. As it rounds the wheel head, the ball effortlessly skips across the depressions like driving over speed bumps. Eventually it will come to rest in one of these indentations.

The Huxley wheels also employ the no-ledge, gradual-escape upper-ball tracks which lengthen the ball's approach to the rotor. Their center cone has a lower incline angle which can temporarily suspend the ball. On the Mark models, cones are almost flush with the rear, or inward portion of the ball-pockets. Not only can the ball skip over the low or no fret pocket walls, it can also exit the rear of the pocket rather easily.

There is an experience that immediately comes to mind when I think of this model wheel. I was mentally tracking a roulette dealer at the Windsor Casino who became very consistent in her last four spins. After confirming the rotor speed and comparing position vectors of the ball to rotor and rotor to a stationery reference point in the bowl, I felt pretty confident that the ball would land in or around the number 7 pocket. I decided to take advantage of the dealer's consistency and place a wager. With only $100 chips in hand, I immediately placed one on the 11, straight up and another on the 17-20 split, covering three numbers within a five-pocket sector. I was decently ahead for the session and felt I had a solid shot at winning some serious money.

Upon seeing my wagers, the dealer called out, "black checks inside." The supervisor walked directly over to observe the event. I became very excited as the ball crossed onto the rotor at the number 9, and entered my 11 pocket, just three pockets later. As I braced myself to celebrate my imminent $3,500 win, I noticed that the ball had exited the rear of my 11 pocket and was now perched on the cone's edge!

I couldn't contain myself, "Fall! Fall! You damned ball!" but it started floating over the 7 pocket. As it worked its way over the 20, I thought, "I'm not greedy, I'll settle for $1,700!" But then it paused right over the 32 pocket, "No-o-o!" I groaned as it plopped down right between the 20 and 17 in the 32 pocket. I fell to my knees and gasped in disbelief.

It wasn't the $200 loss; I was ahead much more than that. It was the teasing, no, *the agony* that this wheel had put me through; first flashing me a small fortune of $3,500, then pulling it back, and then flashing me a $1,700 win, only to pull it back as well. Had the central cone been elevated a little, then the ball wouldn't have had a chance to exit the rear of the 11 pocket, and even if it still did, a more steeply-sloped cone design would have directed the ball back into the pocket. A sympathetic supervisor, realizing exactly how close I came to hitting a big one, handed me a folded slip of paper. It was a $50 comp for one of their nicer restaurants. I appreciated the offer, even though I didn't have much of an appetite. The Huxley wheels provide a formidable challenge, even for the more experienced predictive player.

The TCS Group is another progressive company also based out of London, England. They are a world supplier of live table-game equipment and have manufactured roulette wheels for almost 20 years. TCS manufactures a wheel line known as the Pinnacle. Using a unique ceramic-bearing system developed originally for use in space exploration, the Pinnacle model has moved a step closer to the realm of perpetual motion. The ceramic bearings not only possess lower frictional qualities but also have self-healing properties which free the bearing's raceways of rough particles that will cause premature wear. The wheel's rotor is CNC milled from pressure-cast aluminum at very high tolerances and houses a concentric single-piece separator ring that can be rotated or removed. Separator rings are available in the customary low-fret style or the newer no-fret, scalloped version (which is almost identical to Huxley's Starburst continuous-fret ring). The Pinnacle's rotor assembly was designed with a high security-seal system and can only be accessed with special tools.

The main bowl is built up from continuous rings of MDF board and covered with attractive Italian-wood veneers. Even the upper ball tracks have veneers applied. The ball stops, or canoes, have an elliptical shape and are made from stainless steel. The ball may get past the slender profile of the horizontally positioned deflectors, but because of their height, the ball will definitely be affected if it strikes a vertically oriented canoe. The crowning touch is an ornate turret that is machined from solid aluminum, which is polished, engraved and nickel-plated. These wheels are seductive but dangerous for the advantage player. Like the Huxley wheels, they are optimized for random play, not predictive play, and *random* play achieves the casino's mathematical edge.

Sector Slicing, Carving up the 00 and 0 Wheels

When you first glance at the double-zero wheel head, it appears to be randomly laid out with no particular logic in mind. Actually, a great amount of thought went into its development. The strategy behind laying out the wheel head involves splitting up each betting group as best as possible. By spreading out the major betting groups (dozens, color, high/low, etc.) on the rotor, the game remains closer to random. Keeping the process random is critical to the casino's success because that enforces the casino's mathematical edge. The low and high betting groups on the outside of the layout include numbers 1 to 18 and 19 to 36, respectively, but these are not found consecutively on the wheel itself.

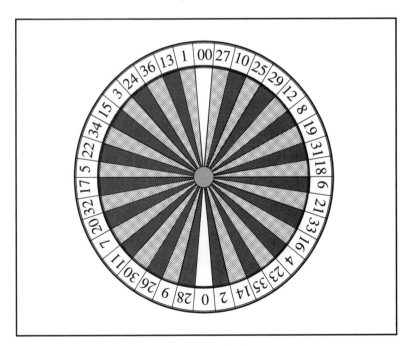

Diagram 3-C
The Double-Zero Wheel

The American Double-Zero Wheel

Look at the wheel-head layout. With the exception of the two zero pockets, each pocket alternates red then black all around the wheel. If you start with the double zero and go counterclockwise, you will observe that there are two low numbers (1, 13) followed by two high numbers (24, 36). This pattern continues . . . (3, 15) then (34, 22), etc. This double alternating pattern persists until just before the 0 and 00 (where a single alternating pattern occurs). You will also note that 1 and 13 are not just low numbers, but they are odd numbers as well. Numbers 24 and 36 are both even, while 3 and 15 are odd again. This odd-even pattern follows a double alternating routine just like the high-low numbers. You will not find more than two highs, lows, odds or evens in a row on the American wheel (zeroes don't count as even). Also, you will not find more than one red or black pocket in a row.

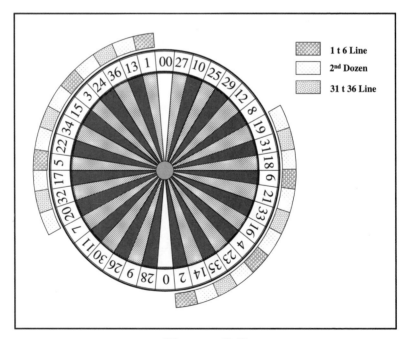

Diagram 3-D
Second Dozen and Neighbors

A strong effort was put into splitting up the other out-side betting groups. The three *dozens* bets and the three *columns* bets pay 2 to 1. The first-dozen bet (numbers 1 through 12) is very well distributed around the rotor. With the exception of the 11 and the 12, they are almost laid out every four pockets apart. The second dozen (numbers 13 through 24) are more polarized. Starting with the 20 and proceeding clockwise, every other number is a black second dozen num-ber: 20, 17, 22, 15, 24 and 13. Conversely, every other number starting with the 19 and heading clockwise is a red second dozen number: 19, 18, 21, 16, 23 and 14. The ball is usually spun clockwise (CW) and the wheel, counterclockwise (CCW). As a result, when it comes upon the region heavily populated with black second dozen numbers, it encounters the 20 first, then the 17 and 22. I often refer to these three numbers as the front-black second dozen. The 15, 24 and 13 are the back-black second dozen. As you might expect, the 19, 18 and 21 are the front-red second dozen and the 16, 23 and 14 pick up the back-red second dozen.

As perfectly as they tried to spread out the groups of numbers on the betting layout, you can see the strategy breaking down a little here. If you take it a step further, you'll notice that the numbers on either side of any second-dozen number is a number contained in either the 1–4 line (numbers 1 through 6) or the 31–34 line (numbers 31 through 36). The black second dozen needs red numbers to alternate with so you will encounter the 32, 5, 34, 3, 36 and 1 sandwiched in between. Conversely, the red second dozen requires black numbers with which to alternate. That is where the 31, 6, 33, 4, 35 and 2 come into the picture. Check out **Diagram 3-D** above. If you wanted to cover all of the pockets in front of the zeroes (going CW), just bet on the 1–4 line, the second dozen numbers and the 31–34 line. If you feel the dealer is hitting this region and are happy with a 50/50 shot (every other number) at tripling your money, then just bet on the second-dozen numbers.

If you know which set of second dozens the dealer will likely hit, you can hone in on that side of the wheel. If, for example, you like the red second dozens, then split the 19-16 and the 18-21. This will give you the front-four red second dozens. If you need to go deeper, just play the 23 and, perhaps, the 14 straight up for two more chips. Another option involves covering the numbers in between. Bet the 4 street (4, 5 and 6) and the 31 street (31, 32 and 33). The underlined numbers are in your sector (the 5 and 32 are extra numbers you will pick up with those street bets). With just four chips you can cover an eight-pocket sector (19 through 4) in the red second-dozen area.

The black second dozen is not much harder to cover. Split the 17-20 with one chip, bet the 13 street (13, 14 and 15) and the 22 street (22, 23 and 24) with two more chips, and you have totally covered the black second dozens with just three

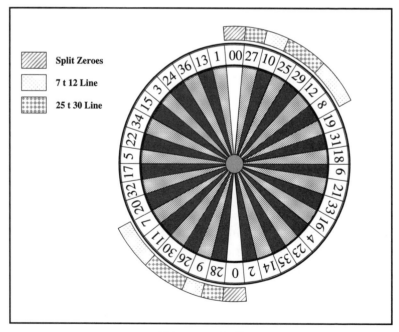

Diagram 3-E
Zeroes and Neighbors

chips. You want the numbers in between covered also? Fine, bet one additional chip on the 1 street (<u>1</u>, 2 and <u>3</u>) and another on the 34 street (<u>34</u>, 35 and <u>36</u>). Again, the underlined numbers are contained in your sector. With the four street bets, you will have an eight-pocket sector covered. When you add the 17-20 split, you will cover 10 numbers out of a 12-pocket sector with five chips. Practice various betting strategies to cover sectors on the wheel. It's a quick and fun way to learn your way around the wheel head!

Going clockwise from the zeroes, three of the next four numbers are third-dozen numbers (00 then 27, 10, 25, 29 and 0 then 28, 9, 26, 30). More specifically, the six numbers immediately after the zeroes (CW) are all contained on the 7–10 line (covers 7 through 12) and the 25–28 line (covers 25 through 30). Look at **Diagram 3-E** for reference. If it looks like the dealer is coming in at or just after the zeroes, then wagering on the 7–10 and 25–28 lines will cover the next six numbers after both zeroes with just two chips. Split the zeroes and possibly the 1-2 if you wish to beef up the front end of this area. If you desire to strengthen the back end of this formation, then split the 19-20 and maybe the 31-32. Again, there are many possibilities. The best thing to do is to obtain a graphic of the wheel head. Then buy a cheap roulette layout like the one depicted in **Diagram 3-F** with some plastic chips and play around with them.

American Roulette Column Distribution

The first-column bet is spread out well over the rotor. It is usually found in blocks of two, with four non–first-column numbers between them (1 and 13 are first-column numbers followed by 36, 24, 3, 15; then 34 and 22 followed by 5, 17, 32 and 20, for example). No more than two first-column numbers can be found in a row. For the second- and third-column numbers, things start to break down more. If we start at number 23 and go CW until we hit number 5, we will have

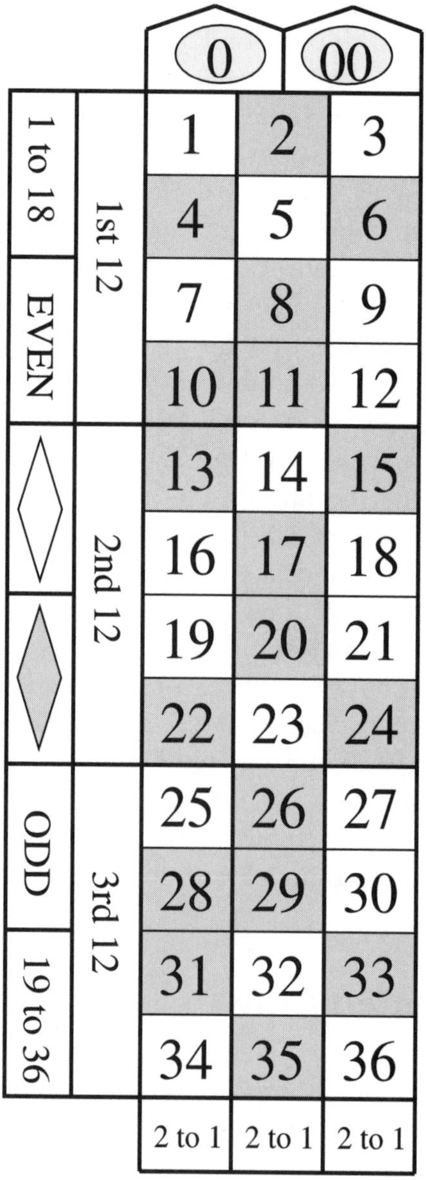

Diagram 3-F
American Double-Zero Table Layout

carved out a 15-number sector centered about number 26. Ten of these numbers, or two-thirds of this sector, are second-column numbers! If you wish to bet on this area, simply place a bet in the second-column box. You can pick up two more non-second-column numbers in this sector by placing a chip on the 28 street (28, 29 and 30). The 28 and 30 are contained in this area. If you really wish to lock up this sector, you can wager on the 7 street (7, 8 and 9), as well. You will pick up two more non–second-column numbers in this area of the rotor for a total of 14 out of 15 or 93.33 percent. Only the single zero is not covered.

The third-column numbers (3, 6, 9, 12, etc.) populate a 19-pocket sector centered about the number 25. Starting with the black 15 and progressing CW to the black 33, 10 of 19 numbers are third-column numbers. Place an additional chip on the 10-13 split to pick up two more non–third-column

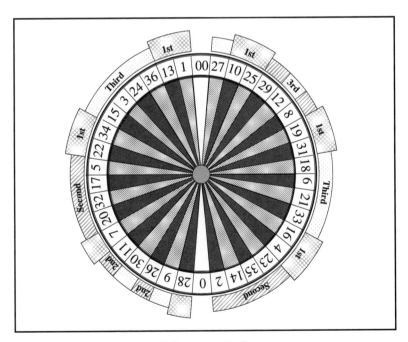

Diagram 3-G
Column Distribution

numbers, increasing your density to 12 out of 19. If the third column comes in, you will win 2 to 1 on your column bet, but lose your 10-13 split netting one unit. If you hit the 10-13 split, you will net 16 units (17 minus 1 on the third column). Incidentally, the number 25 is 180 degrees away from the number 26, so the second and third columns cover opposing halves of the rotor. **Diagram 3-G** shows how the columns are distributed on the American wheel.

Let's discuss individual numbers for a moment. Pick any odd number you like and look for the next highest number (an even number of course). You will notice two things: first, the even number is on the exact opposite side of the wheel (180 degrees away), and second, the even number is always a different color than the odd number. Take number 1, right next to double zero. It's red and odd. The number 2, its counterpart, is black and even. It can be found exactly 19 pockets (180 degrees) away. Start with any odd number and you will encounter the same phenomenon. Now you know the strategy behind laying out the American roulette wheel. Because you will want to observe the spin of the dealer first before wagering (as with any predictive methodology), you also have some techniques for quickly covering wheel sectors with as few chips as possible.

The French Single-Zero Wheel

The French-style wheel layout was devised after the American-style wheel and was introduced in 1842. It is shown in **Diagram 3-H**. The Blanc brothers wanted to boost the popularity of the game by removing one of the zeroes and keeping the payouts the same. They had the right idea, the house edge was nearly cut in half and the game went on to realize new heights in popularity in Europe. They did, however, encounter a problem with the rotor layout. By removing the double zero from the wheel head, two red numbers were now adjacent to each other, the 1 and the 27. Because they wished to keep the betting layout familiar to the players (i.e., the arrangement and colors of each number should remain the same), it became necessary to rearrange the entire wheel head. Unfortunately, the numbers do not appear to be positioned with any particular logic, other than trying to retain the same betting layout and breaking up the major betting groups as best as possible. It looks like the creators went through an iterative process of positioning and repositioning numbers until someone finally declared, "That's good enough."

The outside, even-money numbers are fairly well spread out around the wheel. The red and black numbers alternate perfectly until you reach the green zero that is positioned between the black 26 and the red 32. Both of these numbers, incidentally, are even. Starting just CCW of the 26 with 3, 35 (both odd) and continuing counterclockwise, each block of two numbers alternates even (12, 28), then odd again

Diagram 3-H
The Single-Zero Wheel

(7, 29). This pattern continues down to the 24, where a single alternating pattern begins with an odd 5, even 10 and odd 23. The next two pockets, 8 and 30, are both even, then odd 11 and even 36 follow. A pair of odds appear, then a pair of evens, and then odds again. At no time will you find more than two odds or evens in a row. The low numbers (1 through 18) and the high numbers (19 through 36) occur in a single alternating fashion for the most part. Just counterclockwise of the zero is the high number, 26 followed by the low number 3. This pattern repeats until half way around the wheel where the 5 and 10 (both low numbers) are adjacent to each other. After that, the single alternating pattern picks up again. All of the even-money wagers are fairly well spread out on the wheel.

The first-dozen numbers, for example, can be found with anything from no pockets between them up to five pockets between, the only logic being that the black first-dozen numbers run CW from the zero up to and including the number 10. Conversely, the red first-dozen numbers are CCW of the zero up to and including the number 5. Of all the dozens and columns bets, the second dozen seems to be the most polarized. Starting with the number 15 pocket and proceeding CW until reaching the 18 pocket, you will encounter all 12 of the second-dozen numbers in a 28-pocket sector centered about the 8-30 pockets. You will have three chances in seven to win 2 to 1 if you are sure that the ball will land in this area. The red and black second-dozen numbers are indiscriminately scattered around the wheel. The first number CW from the zero is the black 15. Right next door is the red 19. Two pockets down is the red 21, followed by the black 17 three pockets over, etc. There is no discernible color or spacing pattern present.

The third-dozen numbers are laid out more like the first dozen. There may be anywhere from one to five non–third-dozen pockets in between. The six red third-dozen numbers are CW of the zero to balance out the six black first-dozen numbers found there. Similarly, the black third-dozen numbers neutralize the red first-dozen numbers CCW from the zero.

The first column positioning almost looks like an afterthought. The 19 and 4, as well as the 7 and 28, are pairs of first-column numbers directly adjacent to each other. There are three occurrences where only one pocket separates two first-column numbers and five where two non–first-column numbers are in between. Then it jumps up to five non–first-column numbers between the 10 and 13 and seven pockets between the 19 and 28. The red or black first-column numbers do not follow any particular order or lie in any certain area of the rotor. The numbers in this group are located in a very irregular fashion. The second-column numbers are scattered a little better, with no pockets, one pocket, three pockets, four pockets or five pockets in between them at different points. They look more like smaller clusters scattered about. Again, the second-column red and black colors are spread around with no pattern in mind.

Of all the columns, the third column is the most evenly distributed of the groups. You will find zero, one, two, three or four pockets containing non–third-column numbers between them. None of the columns can be used to play a particular region of the wheel head.

The Advancing 3 Split Bets

Using several *cheval*, or split bets, it is possible to cover certain parts of the French wheel head. There are two opposing halves that you can cover using a technique I've dubbed "The Advancing Splits." One sector is centered at the number 3, just two pockets CCW from 0. This sector actually starts off around the 26 and shifts to the 3. Place the splits in the order that I give them to you and you will start at the center and advance your way outward.

1. Place the 26 straight up.
2. Split the 0-3; you now have a three-pocket sector covered.
3. Split the 32-35; you now have a five-pocket sector.
4. Split the 12-15; you now have a seven-pocket sector
5. Split the 28-29; you now have 9 out of 10 pockets.
6. Split the 4-7; you now have 11 out of 12.
7. Split the 18-21; you now have 13 numbers in a 14-pocket sector.
8. Split 19-22; you now have a complete 15-pocket sector covered.

You probably won't have time to place all eight chips, but you will start at the center and spread further out with each wager that you are able to place. Refer to **Diagram 3-I** for further details.

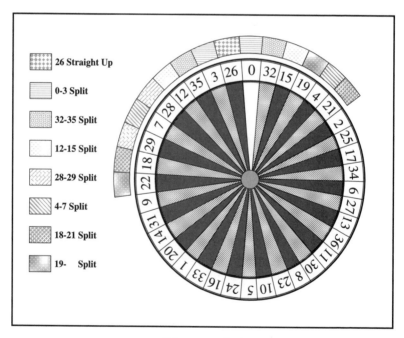

Diagram 3-I
The Advancing 3 Splits

The Advancing 30 Split Bets

This set of splits covers the sector centered about the number 30. Again, place them in the order shown below if you wish to advance or expand outward from the number 30. **Diagram 3-J** shows which area of the rotor you are covering with these wagers.

1. Split the 8-11; 2 numbers in a 3-pocket sector.
2. Split the 10-13; 4 numbers in a 7-pocket sector.
3. Split the 27-30; 6 numbers in an 8-pocket sector.
4. Split the 5-6; 8 numbers in a 10-pocket sector.
5. Split the 23-24; 10 numbers in an 11-pocket sector.
6. Split the 33-36; 12 numbers in a 13-pocket sector.
7. Split the 16-17; 14 numbers in a 15-pocket sector.

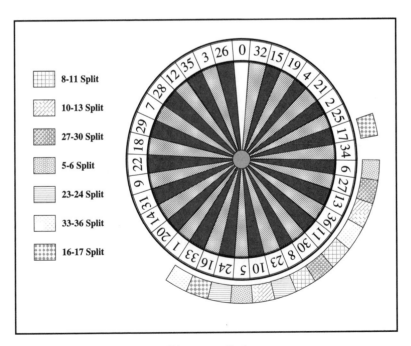

Diagram 3-J
The Advancing 30 Splits

You may not get all seven chips out before the dealer waves off the betting, but don't worry. With both of these betting techniques, locate and practice placing the first three bets described. Once you can execute these quickly and accurately, then add one extra bet and practice until you are proficient. Continue to add one at a time until you can cover the entire region. When you are able to cover the entire region, you will have a few options open to you. With the French wheels, you will usually find higher table minimums. If, for example, the minimum is $25, then you may want to cover the first five bets in the advancing splits. With five $5 chips, you will satisfy the minimum betting requirements.

Let us say that the minimum chip value that you can wager is a whopping $25. You may not want to bet more than $50 per spin. Place just the first two bets in the outline for $25 each. For the Advancing 3, you would play the 26 straight up, then split the 0-3. For the Advancing 30 technique, you would split the 8-11 and the 10-13. Look at the table minimums and decide what your unit size will be. Then determine the number of chips, or units per round, you will wager. Only bet on spins that you think are directed near the center of these sectors. Otherwise, you will have to get proficient at betting five chips in a tight five-pocket sector to cover various areas on the rotor.

The 180 Plays

Sometimes the dealer bounces back and forth across the wheel. You may have a good idea what area that he is going into, however, sometimes he hits on the exact opposite side, or 180 degrees away. Depending on the dealer and the wheel speed, this may be an occasional or frequent occurrence. I will show you a couple of techniques for simultaneously covering two sectors that are 180 degrees away from each other.

The '11-12' 180 Play

This play covers two opposing sectors. One is roughly centered about the number 11. The other is centered near the number 12 pocket. Place the splits in this order for maximum effectiveness:

1. Split the 11-12
2. Split the 7-8
3. Split the 35-36
4. Split the 23-26

If you have more time, you can . . .

5. Split the 10-13
6. Split the 0-3
7. Split the 28-29
8. Split the 27-30

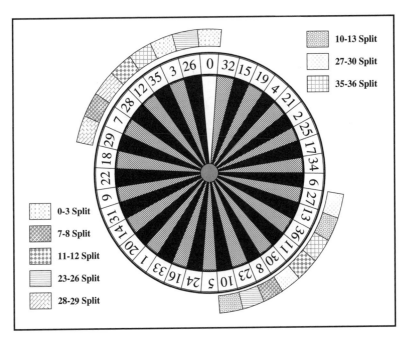

Diagram 3-K
The '11–12' 180 Degree Play

You will have two opposing quarters with eight pockets each covered. If, on the other hand you are pressed for time, you can play two reduced sectors very quickly. Wager the 10 street (covers 10, 11 and 12), the 28 street (covers 28, 29 and 30) and the 7-8 split. If you experiment a little, you will discover other combinations. Look at **Diagram 3-K** for an illustration of the eight split bets described above.

The '14-17' 180 Play

This play covers two opposing sectors that are sandwiched in between the previous two sectors centered about the 11 and 12 pockets. Again, follow the order given below:

1. Split the 31-34
2. Split the 22-25
3. Split the 20-21
4. Split the 14-17

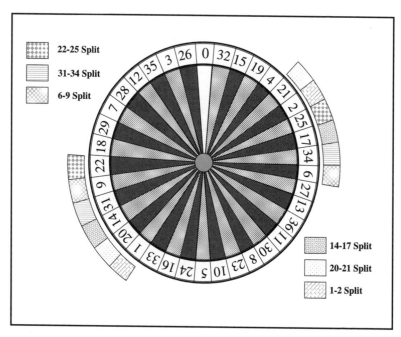

Diagram 3-L
The '14–17' 180 Degree Play

5. Split the 6-9

6. Split the 1-2

There are only six chips to bet, so we will start at the high end of the betting layout (31–34) and sweep across through the midsection (22–25, 20–21 and 14–17). Then we will finish up with the lower numbers (6–9 and 1–2). **Diagram 3-L** portrays the opposing sectors covered with these bets. Don't be afraid to try some different betting combinations for yourself. The combinations that I've shared with you here in this section are the most powerful ones that I've uncovered. In lieu of strictly betting five-pocket sectors, they have served me well at the tables.

If you are inclined to, you can memorize the American or French rotor layout. Once you have accomplished that, you can practice spreading five or seven chips, centered about your target number, corresponding to a particular sector on the rotor. You will need to practice this over a partially covered betting layout because the other players will probably wager before the dealer spins. You will only have two or three seconds to get your bets down after making your prediction and before the dealer cries, "No more bets." I usually load both hands up and simultaneously position my stakes on both ends of the layout. If you can consistently get to the numbers on the betting layout and wager your wheel sector in about two seconds, then you are well on your way. You will have mastered the betting portion of professional play. This minor feat took me about 50 hours worth of practice time to perfect.

The betting techniques that I covered earlier in this section aren't quite as thorough as betting a single chip on each number in your sector; however, they can be learned in only two to three hours. In addition, these bets can be placed in half the time or less, making the betting more efficient and allowing a little more time to ensure an accurate prediction.

To further assist with practicing wagering strategies and quick bet placement, you should obtain a roulette card from the casino or order Joe Zanghi's reusable plastic *Action Play Roulette Tracker Card*. Carry it around with you. You can put it in a shirt pocket or some other convenient place on your person. Whenever you find that you have a few minutes of time to kill, pull out the diagram and study it. After a few weeks or so, test yourself. Make a blank circle with 38 slices (or 37 if you plan on playing the French-style wheel) and try to fill them in by memory. Work first for accuracy, then build on speed. You now know the logic that was used to create the wheel's layout, so you will be able to deduce where certain numbers or groups of numbers are located. The goal here is to have an idea of what numbers are located in what areas.

If you are planning on using wheel watching or visual-tracking techniques, then you must have the whole wheel layout down cold. You should be able to close your eyes and see the wheel head, with the ability to quickly call out all of the numbered pockets sequentially, starting at any number and going either CW or CCW. Once you know what your target number and its neighbors are, you will then find yourself playing twister on the betting layout to cover them. This level of mastery is not necessary for the serious part-time player, but such a player should at least know his way around the wheel.

Part 4

Techniques Used by Professionals

Professional Roulette Play

If I told you, "We're going to a place that's crowded. People are rude. They'll bump into you, knock you aside, blow cigar smoke in your face and every hour or so someone will reach into your pocket and take a couple of hundred bucks," I'm sure you'd look at me incredulously. But what if I said, "Hey, have you been over to the casino lately?" You might reply, "No. Let's go!"

We cannot do anything about the other casino patrons, be they rude or crude, but we can cut down on the money that leaves our pockets and maybe even make a few bucks. If you frequent the gambling halls, then it pays to be knowledgeable, even skillful, at reading and exploiting certain situations that develop at the roulette tables. This section and the one to follow will explore how to achieve just that. By the end of this section, you will have a good idea what the masters of the game do to obtain their edge. In the next section I will offer some practical approaches for the serious part-time player.

Now that we have a good idea of what transpires during a single roulette trial, we are in a better position to understand the advantage systems used by professional players. There are two expert-level systems that read and take advantage of the physical phenomena controlling the game of roulette.

Biased wheel play requires tireless hours of wheel clocking, some statistical analysis and repeatedly betting on the same number(s). It seeks out and exploits wheels that are biased, those that tend to favor a particular number or group of numbers. Wheel tracking is more difficult to master as it requires much study and practice, some scouting and the ability to recognize patterns between the spinning ball and the rotating wheel head. The tracker must execute split-second analyses and immediate bet placements. There are not many people worldwide who are capable of employing this second system.

I have also included a short description of a third methodology that has some technical merit. However, I do not know of anyone using this "theoretical" technique to make serious money.

Wheel Tracking

To give the reader a basic idea, the wheel tracker analyzes the mechanical conditions of each roulette spin and formulates a prediction based on those conditions. The system calls for the player to study the speed of the rotating ball relative to that of the wheel head, which spins in the opposite direction. The intersection points of the ball with, for example, the single-zero pocket are compared to a stationery point in the bowl. As these intersection points drift (because the ball decelerates much faster than the rotor) the player is keying into a particular revolution before the ball breaks from the upper track. At that revolution, position vectors are quickly observed and evaluated. That same revolution must be selected from trial to trial so that the player may adjust his prediction slightly, similar to the way artillerymen calculate the trajectory of a shell onto a designated surface. At that critical moment, a prediction is formulated and wagers are placed with lightning speed.

An Early Wheel Tracker

"One of the most spectacular and popular gamblers at Monte Carlo," wrote Russell Barnhart in his book *Beating the Wheel*, "was a handsome young American named William Nelson Darnborough from Bloomington, Illinois. How he beat roulette at Monte Carlo from 1904 to 1911 has been a well-kept secret." Darnborough, in fact, beat the casino to the extent of $415,000. A sum, no doubt, equal to 10 or 15 times that amount in today's dollars.

An eyewitness, the honorable S. R. Beresford, wrote in his 1926 memoirs: "An American named Darnborough enriched himself to the extent of 83,000 pounds from the Monte Carlo Casino alone. He undoubtedly broke all records for continuous gain. Mr. Darnborough was probably the most remarkable man, so far as gambling is concerned, that ever passed into the casino at Monte Carlo. Never before or since have such masses of gold and notes been heaped upon a roulette table. The most astonishing feature of his operation was the lightning speed with which he placed his stakes. He would commence staking his money when the croupier commenced to spin, continuing to dab the board with piles of money . . . His masses in reserve encroached on the board itself." Who was this dashing American who disappeared as mysteriously as he first appeared in Monte Carlo? What system was he using to beat this game?

Darnborough, according to Russel Barnhart, was born in Bloomington, Illinois, in 1868. After graduating from Illinois State Normal University, he boarded a train headed for St. Louis, Missouri to play semiprofessional baseball. Darnborough was an outstanding athlete, with almost abnormally keen vision, but after two years, new vistas beckoned. He purchased a saloon in Chicago with the money he had earned as a pitcher. Darnborough set up a roulette wheel in the back room of his bar, which was considered standard issue for a Chicago saloon in the 1880s. Then one evening an anonymous gentlemen entered the saloon, sat down to play roulette, and began to win.

The two battled it out all night, Darnborough with his undersized bank and the stranger with his growing resources. By dawn, both men were physically and emotionally spent. However, there was one noticeable difference, the stranger had won had every penny Darnborough had. Darnborough proposed to the stranger, "We'll spin the wheel one more time. If red comes up, all the money you've won tonight will be mine again. If black comes up, you'll own my entire saloon." The stranger agreed. The ball was spun and finally came to rest. It was black.

William Darnborough bid farewell to his staff and walked through the saloon doors one final time to see what adventure the world had in store for him next. He joined a traveling circus, drawing extra money from his unerring pitching ability. As the circus was making its way through the southwest, Darnborough became disenchanted and left one night. Aside from his horse, he acquired a companion named Charlie and a small roulette wheel, whose mechanical laws he studied carefully. Darnborough was hell-bent on conquering and exploiting the very game that financially ruined him.

Whenever he was able to, he set up his wheel and banked a game. There was a big difference this time, though. The mid-westerner knew what he doing. Darnborough became so proficient that he accepted challenges to play at saloons containing their own roulette wheels—and seldom lost. By the time he had traveled down to Mexico, his name preceded him. "The American is coming!" went the cry, and a roulette wheel was set up for Darnborough and his companion. Gamblers and speculators alike began to ask themselves:

had Darnborough figured out a system that could beat roulette?

According to Barnhart, the two men traveled through Central America, Columbia, Ecuador, over the Andes by mule and finally to Peru. The two eventually made their way back to the states after what was a long and difficult journey, but Darnborough had only begun. In his mid-thirties, William Darnborough purchased a ticket and sailed for Europe. He played cards and roulette in private clubs throughout Amsterdam, Paris and London.

The accomplished gambler was on the scene in Monte Carlo by 1904. By 1911, he was some $415,000 ahead from playing roulette there. To put an ending to the story, William courted and married a beautiful, young English woman, swore off gambling to satisfy her family and settled down in the English countryside.

Was this man incredibly lucky, or had he discovered an amazing system for beating the game? It should be noted that Darnborough beat the casino consistently, and over a great stretch of time. This was not luck. The approach that Mr. Darnborough used around the dawn of the 20th century, I believe, was based upon classical physics. It is the most powerful way to conquer the game of roulette, but it is probably the most difficult to learn and employ. Barnhart refers to this method as *wheel watching*. It has been dubbed *visual tracking* or something of the like by others.

Working with a Modern Wheel Tracker

There is another wheel watcher mentioned in Barnhart's book. He is a modern-day player who heads up a software development company in the southwest. This intelligent and unassuming man writes under the name of Laurance Scott (not his full name). I was lucky—and persuasive—enough to have Mr. Scott, whom I consider to be the world's foremost authority on the topic, take me under his

wing and fill in some of the missing pieces I needed to be successful at wheel tracking. My background in two engineering
disciplines, experience with computers and my appetite for
devouring all available material on the subject, helped me to
gain a solid understanding of the physical phenomena
involved.

Newtonian physics, its governing laws of gravity and
its equations of planetary motion describe why the little white
ball hovers in orbit for a time, then spirals down to meet the
much larger, constantly spinning wheel head. Even after
understanding the impetus for what was unfolding, and
reading Scott's detailed notes three times, it took me nine
months to be able to effectively apply this system in actual
play. I would compare the difficulty of employing this system
to using a 3-level, side of aces, full-strategy indices, count
adjustment for betting size, expert level blackjack system, taking up to 1000+ hours of practice to master. There is no way
that I can teach you everything about wheel tracking in one
section of a book, or even at all, for that matter, but I would
like you to understand the basic logic behind it all.

Those of you interested in serious wheel watching will
now have a starting point. In addition, the approach that we
will discuss in **Part 5** has its underpinnings in this methodology. I have taught various clinics on gambling in Atlantic
City, Reno and Las Vegas. With regards to the game of
roulette, we always seem to gravitate towards a more practical approach, based upon dealer's bias or signature.
However, I do not want to dissuade the determined. So let us
start by taking a look at what the *wheel tracker* or *wheel watcher* is doing up to and including the point where he places his
bets. Then we will take a more detailed look into the actual
mechanical conditions, primarily the patterns that develop
between the ball and the spinning numbered rotor. After that,
we will revisit the description of what the wheel tracker is
looking for and how the predictions are made. For those suf-

ficiently inclined to further study, I will provide you with a list of publications at the end of this section.

What a Wheel Tracker Does

Let's talk about what a wheel tracker is doing on a basic level. The wheel tracker must first scout and find a wheel/dealer combination that is playable before deciding to wager. I will elaborate on ideal playing conditions a little later. The croupier, or dealer, gives the wheel a little CCW kick with the pinky and ring fingers to build the speed back up and then releases the ball in the CW direction. At this point, the wheel tracker will begin assessing the spin. He will first gauge the speed of the wheel head and check for consistency with previous spins. If consistent, he will begin to take position vectors, comparing the ball's declining speed to that of the constantly spinning rotor. The ball's rate of velocity diminishes rapidly because of gravity, rolling friction, wind resistance and other factors.

At one critical point, a few revolutions before the ball drops off the upper track, the wheel tracker will evaluate the position of the rotating ball with that of the spinning rotor in one region of the stationery bowl and make a prediction. At this juncture, he now has maybe two or three seconds to get his bets out on the layout. Many times the wheel tracker is engaged in a twister-like game of bet placements under the sweeping arm of the dealer crying, "No-o more bets!"

The tracker will typically lose on more spins then he will win, but when he does win, it will more than make up for his loses. For example, a wheel tracker playing a five-pocket wheel sector must hit at least once in every seven trials. In this situation, the tracker will lose five units on six spins, which equals 30 units lost. On the one spin that hits, he will lose four more units but will keep the one unit that won. That one unit will collect 35 units for a straight up hit. The wheel tracker's net gain, in this case, is 35 units won minus 34 units lost, or +1 unit. The tracker wins one time in seven attempts, but continues to grind his way up.

Likewise, a tracker, or any bettor for that matter, must win one attempt in five if he plans on covering a seven-pocket sector. He will lose four times seven plus six for a total of −34 units. The one win yields him +35 units for a net of +1 unit. One hit every twelve spins for a three pocket sector would break even or net 0 units as would one hit every three spins for a twelve pocket sector. You can work out other win-to-sector length ratios for yourself.

"What, exactly, is the wheel tracker tracking?" you ask. Well, let's back up a little first. There are three questions that the tracker must be able to answer before rendering a prediction:

1. Which section of the upper track will the ball drop from?

2. When will the ball drop off?

3. What sector of the rotor will be there to greet the ball after it drops?

The first question will be answered later when we talk about scouting. You will essentially scout for wheels with consistent drop-off points. The second and third questions can be answered by studying the unfolding patterns that occur during a roulette spin. This is what the wheel tracker is tracking and analyzing.

When the ball is first spun, it travels much faster than the rotor (in the opposite direction). As discussed earlier in this section, the ball's rate of velocity breaks down very fast because of various factors, while the more massive rotor can spin at the same rate for an extended period of time. As a result, the ball starts out much faster than the wheel, slows down rather rapidly and, at some consistent angular-velocity threshold, gravity will pull it from the upper track. Regardless of how fast the ball starts out, it will continue to spin until it slows to a specific *exit velocity*. If the relative position of the ball to the rotor could be evaluated consistently at, say, three revolutions before this moment in the spin (denoted by T – 3 revolutions) then the velocity would be the same at this point in time also. Now you have a specific ball velocity that can be compared to a constant wheel velocity. A prediction can be made based on both the ball's and rotor's position relative to some stationary observation point in the bowl. You will now have, maybe, a couple of seconds to place your bets.

Determining the Wheel's Angular Velocity

By now you probably realize that a constant wheel velocity is imperative to seeing consistent and predictable ball-to-wheel formations. Just after the ball is released, you will time one rotor revolution. Select a vertical ball deflector that is clearly visible from your vantage point. After the dealer kicks the wheel speed back up (just before releasing the ball), watch for the single zero. As soon as it passes under your diamond deflector, begin your count. When your count is complete, observe the number that is directly under your vertical deflector. That is your wheel-speed index number. You do not need to convert this to an actual angular velocity. Just remember it for that particular playing session.

On subsequent spins, you will time the rotor right after the ball is released to ensure that this index number hasn't changed. If this wheel speed index number is the same from trial to trial, then you have a croupier who rotates the wheel head at a constant angular velocity (wheel speed is the same).

Let me explain what I mean by the count. We will use a count of sorts to time the rotor. I have trained myself to count to ten in exactly two seconds. I use this as my timing method. The two seconds is not so important. It is the consistency of your timing method. I have subsequently found that using a cadence or song fragment is easier to employ. For example, the single zero passes under your chosen deflector . . . you begin to sing a snippet of that classic by the Kingsmen to yourself . . . "Louie Lou-i-i-e, boom-boom," stop, and you notice that the number 6 is under your deflector when you conclude the cadence. That's it! Your wheel speed index number is 6. Only play wheels with the same rotor velocity (consistent wheel-speed index number).

Some trackers have tried using a stopwatch to index wheel speeds, but it can be difficult to operate one in the heat of the battle. You are better off quietly counting or chanting some short cadence to yourself that you can consistently duplicate after each spin. For each wheel speed, there will be a different set of ball-to-rotor formations. It is not practical to try to memorize 38 sets of formations for 38 different index numbers. Besides, each wheel/ball combination would require discovering and remembering a whole new set of formations.

The easiest thing to do is index the rotor speed and compare it with the previous spin. If the index number is different, then take a walk. Otherwise, stay and play. After you see the same formations from the same wheel speed, you will begin to recognize them more readily. You will only need to keep one running set of calculations once you know that the rotor speed is constant from trial to trial. Surprisingly, over 90 percent of the dealers that I have encountered automatically kick the wheel speed right back up to where it was on the previous ball snap. Usually they have to make a conscious effort to change it up. We do not need to calculate the rotor's angular velocity, but we do need a test that will show timing consistency from one trial to the next.

The Crossover Patterns

"How can you pinpoint a T − 3, or any other specific ball revolution before drop off?" you inquire. This is a key area where Laurance Scott helped me. I realized that a particular visual pattern occurred with faster spinning rotors when the ball's speed approached that of the rotor's. With moderate to slower wheels, however, this pattern does not have a chance to unfold before gravity will pull the ball out from the upper track. "There is a similar pattern that almost always occurs," Scott explained, "when the ball slows down to twice the speed of the wheel."

He went on to describe what he calls, the crossover patterns. The 2-X crossover pattern occurs when the ball slows down to twice the speed of the rotor. The 1-X crossover pattern occurs when the ball slows down to the same speed as that of the rotor. What is so special about these velocity relationships? They are visually easy to spot and for a constant wheel velocity, they occur at the same point in the spin's history. Because the ball starts out much faster than the wheel, the 2-X crossover will occur first. As the ball continues to slow, the 1-X crossover will come about three or four revolutions later. If the rotor is spinning sufficiently slowly, the ball will never reach the 1-X crossover pattern. The ball's exit velocity will override and the ball will be pulled down by gravity before the pattern can develop. That is why Mr. Scott recommended using the 2-X pattern to gauge a specific "T – n" ball revolution.

Depending upon the rotor speed administered by the dealer, the 2-X crossover can occur two revolutions or up to eight revolutions before the ball drops from the upper track. If the rotor speed is constant from trial to trial, then the 2-X crossover will always occur on the same T – n ball revolution. If the 2-X occurs at T – 6 or earlier, then the 1-X crossover should probably be used to reference the T – 3 or T – 2 revolution (whichever the case will be). Otherwise, the tracker will use the 2-X pattern to mark a later revolution (probably in the T – 5 to T – 2 range).

I would recommend making the prediction at the T – 4, to T – 3 ball revolution range. At this point, you can get an accurate enough reading (the later the evaluation, the more accurate) as well as having just enough time to get three or four bets down. If the 2-X occurs at T – 5, wait one or two ball revolutions so you are in the T – 4 to T – 3 range, and then evaluate the rotor's position to some stationary observation point. You will make your prediction at this point in the spin's history.

"But how do you recognize the crossover patterns?" you ask. Let me take you through just how these patterns develop and you will understand how to look for them. As the ball is circling in a clockwise direction in the upper track of the stationary bowl, the numbered rotor is spinning counterclockwise. If you select a reference point on the rotor, such as the single zero, you can notice such times that the ball (CW direction) and the single zero (CCW direction) will align with each other. That means the vectors defining their paths will intersect. (If you have difficulty seeing the intersections, focus a little more on the green 0 and see if you can spot when the ball races by with your peripheral vision.) If the ball and the wheel align at zero degrees (or any starting point you reference), and then again 180 degrees later, and finally back at their starting point 360 degrees later, then for that moment, they are traveling at the same speed.

Think about it. They intersect right in front of the dealer, for example. Because they are traveling at the same rate of speed, they will both reach the opposite side (180 degrees away) and back again in front of the dealer at the same time. This is how we track the ratio of ball speed to rotor speed. This ratio of speeds is constantly changing with the ball decelerating much faster than the rotor, but the pattern should be apparent for one complete ball revolution.

Now envision a ball circling faster than the wheel head, which is typically the case at the beginning of the spin. Because the ball is moving faster initially, it will cover more ground than the rotor. The ball may start out eight or ten times faster than the rotor. At some point, perhaps midway through the spin, the wheel will cover 90 degrees (1/4 of revolution) before it next aligns with the ball. That means the ball had to travel 270 degrees (3/4 of a revolution) to reach that point, coming from the opposite direction. The ball, covering

270 degrees, was spinning three times faster than the rotor that covered only 90 degrees in the same amount of time. The ball will intersect the single zero five times with this difference in velocities; once at zero degrees, then again at 90, 180, 270 and finally 360 degrees of the wheel's revolution.

As the ball slows down, an interesting thing happens. The angle of intersection increases causing the point of alignment to drift in a CCW direction. On the next pass, the wheel may rotate 120 degrees before encountering the ball, still rotating in the upper track. Now the ball has only covered 240 degrees before aligning with our single zero. The ball is now traveling twice as fast as the rotor. This is where the 2-X crossover pattern occurs.

You can observe the 2-X crossover by watching for the ball and single zero to intersect at some starting point (we will call this 0 degrees), 120 degrees later in the CCW direction (from the wheel's perspective), 240 degrees later yet and finally 360 at the same starting point. The ball will have traveled 720 degrees in the CW direction. You will have to watch the entire bowl inside of the wheel to see all of the intersections. You will also have to develop a very good visual feel for judging the ball-to-single-zero formations every 120 degrees (rotor's perspective). In addition to this, you will need to make an observation at some predetermined point in the bowl, the moment the 2-X pattern concludes, then make some quick calculations before betting. All of this can be a bit overwhelming for a mere mortal!

Luckily for me (and you), Laurance Scott was willing to share his technique for tracking the 2-X crossover. Instead of trying to follow the single zero-to-ball intersections all around the wheel, trying to pinpoint 120-degree sectors, he has a method whereby the alignments occur at the same place in the bowl. Select a one-third, or 120-degree slice of the bowl that is situated before the ball's drop-off octant. This will be your primary place to view the 2-X crossover alignment and observation number needed for making the prediction. As you notice that the 2-X pattern is imminent, you will focus on this segment of the bowl. As the pattern begins to develop, let us say the single 0 aligns with the ball in your 120 degree segment, instead of following the 0 and ball around the wheel every 120 degrees, you will focus on the intersection point in your 120-degree bowl segment where the single 0 and ball first aligned. As the ball comes back around (one full ball revolution), the 00 will approach from the opposite direction (one-half wheel revolution). They should intersect at this same point in our 120-degree segment of the roulette bowl.

Now, continue to watch as the ball circles around one more time, completing the second revolution. The single 0 will come back into the picture (completing one full rotor revolution) and they will align very nearly with their original crossing on the previous passing. This completes the 2-X crossover pattern. At this time, you will make your observation (more on that later). So, with Scott's method, you are watching both the single- and double-zero alignments with the ball to gauge the 2-X crossover. This technique is easier to execute because you are monitoring one intersection point instead of three. Also, the chance of error is reduced because you are comparing everything to that one specific point. By the way, it may have turned out, depending on that particular wheel speed, that the 00, 0 and 00 formation will have caused the 2-X crossover instead of the 0, 00, 0. This is fine. Just select the zero formation that best fits the pattern's timing and stick to it for that particular session (with the same wheel velocity).

As the ball continues to slow, the frequency of ball-to-single-zero alignments decrease per wheel revolution and the angle from one alignment to the next gets larger. The alignment, where the ball and single zero intersect, continues to drift CCW. Eventually, the ball will slow down to the same speed as the wheel head. At this moment in time, the intersection point stops drifting. They will intersect only three times, the fewest number possible. This will happen at some point we will call 0 degrees, 180 degrees further and again at 360 degrees. Now, because the ball's speed continues decreasing rapidly, the point of alignment between the ball and the single zero will start drifting clockwise. The intersection point will drift CW at a faster pace as the wheel's speed remains constant and the ball slows down considerably. The ball never stops completely in the upper track because gravity will pull it down the conical incline. The sequence of revolutions will unfold as described above with one overriding parameter— gravity. If the rotor is spinning too slowly, the 1-X crossover will not get the opportunity to unfold. This is because a ball speed equal to that of the rotor's will be too slow to sustain the ball in the upper track against gravity's pull.

You can practice looking for these crossover patterns. Find a moderate to faster spinning rotor and see if you can spot the 1-X crossover (ball-to-single zero formation). After you get comfortable with this pattern, move on to a slower rotor and practice observing the more difficult 2-X crossover pattern (ball-to-both-zeroes formation). You will probably use the 2-X pattern more than 90 percent of the time. If you are serious about wheel tracking, review the section on crossover patterns until you can visualize this phenomenon in your mind's eye.

Spotting the Observation Number

The 2-X crossover pattern provides you with a consistent point in time to make a critical observation. This observation will lead to your prediction. In that same 120-degree segment of the bowl where you saw the 2-X pattern unfold, you will select a stationary point to use as a reference. A vertical ball deflector near the center of your 120-degree bowl segment will probably work well for this. Just as the last alignment is made in the 2-X crossover, you will glimpse at the number directly below your stationary observation point. This number is your observation number.

The observation number is important because it relates a certain position of the spinning rotor to the anticipated drop-off octant at a particular moment in the spin's history. If the observation number is 5, for example, and the ball breaks from the anticipated track octant, then you can note the number under the ball when it begins to leave the upper track.

Let's say that this number, under the ball drop, happens to be 00. The ball will spiral down the apron, while the rotor continues to turn in the opposite direction. The ball may strike, or cross onto the rotor around the single 0, bounce forward eight or nine pockets, and come to rest in the 5 pocket. This would be ideal, because the 5 was also our observation number.

If the 2 becomes our observation number on the next spin, with the same wheel speed, then it will also be our predicted number for that trial. You will bet on the 2, and its neighbors, after making your observation. Most times, things do not work out this neatly. You can adjust your point of observation within the 120-degree segment, to align with the predicted number, or any easy-to-add portion of the wheel from it, if you feel inclined to do so. Assuming a manageable ball bounce, you can relate the resulting number that hit back to the observation number. Use this relative position, or number of pockets, to predict the final number from the observed number.

Scouting for the Right Playing Conditions

The wheel tracker must be aware of the wheel types used in the casinos he frequents. Does the upper race have a more pronounced lip or ledge to better hold the ball right up until the time gravity sends it down to the rotor? This makes predicting easier because the ball's path is more direct with much less room for error. Or, does the upper track blend right in with the apron, such that the ball gradually escapes? The ball will spiral halfway around the wheel, probably hitting several deflectors before striking the rotor.

Speaking of ball deflectors, are they larger (bad) or of the smaller variety (better)? Does the wheel have deep frets (pocket separators)? The deeper the frets, the better the chance of capturing the ball sooner. Perhaps the wheel is the latest model with a continuous fret ring. This is the worst kind to play for any method. Watch to see how lively the ball is after it enters the rotor. The ball bounce must be manageable or you cannot gain any positive edge. Does the dealer change roulette balls on alternate spins? Or does the casino employ only one ball size and material? Playing against a dealer who alternates a 3/4" nylon ball with a 5/8" acetate ball, for example, means that you must maintain two sets of data in your mind. Does the dealer keep the wheel at both a moderate and consistent speed from trial to trial? Dealers may be instructed to vary wheel speeds and sometimes are required to spin the wheel in alternating directions from one spin to the next.

On a recent visit to Las Vegas at the Luxor Casino, I was doing quite well at one of the roulette tables. The dealer began using two different roulette balls. I proved my proficiency at keeping two running sets of data in my head, so he began to spin the wheel clockwise on the third and fourth spins. Up to this point I had doubled my initial buy-in, but now I was doing my best to tread water.

Out of frustration, I asked the dealer why he was going through all this trouble to mix things up; after all, I was tipping generously enough. His face turned a little red and, before he could say anything, a boss piped up (seemingly out of nowhere) and explained that he is just following the casino's procedures. Instead of arguing the point, I colored in and cashed out. Eventually, the casinos will throw enough hurdles at you if they want to. No wheel tracker is good enough to overcome them all. Each variable they introduce will reduce your edge by increasing your chance for error. If the dealers begin to mix things up on you, or start to call off the betting a little earlier each spin, then pack it in. Your bankroll will thank you.

One additional factor that bears mentioning is the amount of wheel tilt. A tilted wheel actually makes roulette prediction easier because the tracker knows where the ball will tend to break, or drop from the upper race. As the ball climbs up to the apex of the tilt, it is working harder against gravity. The chances of the ball making it up to the top of the tilt diminish with each circling pass. The more that the whole roulette wheel is tilted, the higher the frequency of ball drops from that octant of the wheel containing the tilt's apex. A defect in the upper ball track may have a similar effect. Each time the ball passes, some minute obstruction may cause it to slow down at a faster rate. Eventually, the ball will be traveling too slow to overcome the defect and will be tripped out of the upper track. This will result in more ball departures from the track just after the defect.

You can track the octant frequency of ball drops for yourself. Break the bowl up into octants, separated by the silver deflectors. Pick the octant directly in front of the dealer and mentally label it as octant one. Follow along clockwise and number each octant until you come upon the eighth and final one.

On the back of your roulette card, label columns 1 through 8. Watch 20 ball drops initially and record which upper track octant each one fell from by putting an X under that octant's number. If 10 or more of the 20 drops came from the same half of the wheel track, then you may have a playable situation. Continue to chart another 80 ball drops to confirm this, otherwise abandon that wheel and check the next one. Just as a side note, practice looking for the crossover patterns as you chart all these ball drops. After 100 ball drops, you will have created an octant drop histogram. Look for a wheel with about 40 percent or more of its ball drops coming off one octant. Such a wheel may have as much as 1/4" of tilt or a defective upper track situation. This presents the best chance for wheel tracking success.

It is possible to visually track wheels that are not overly inclined, but the skill level needed in reading the subtleties of the patterns may go beyond the perception of the most human beings. Besides, if you know where the ball will likely drop from, then you have greatly simplified the problem. You will only need to calculate when the ball will break and what sector of the wheel will be there to greet the ball. As we discussed earlier, proper evaluation of the crossover patterns will answer these two questions.

Through the Eyes of the Tracker

After the tracker is confident that he has an edge for a particular situation, he will approach the table to buy in and get a closer look. The wheel tracker may work with an accomplice. The accomplice, who must have the wheel's layout thoroughly memorized, will place the bets. The tracker, who studies the rotating wheel and relative ball movement, will make the predictions. The tracker will stand by the wheel so that he has a full view of the wheel and his betting accomplice. The accomplice needs to be positioned so that he can reach most, if not all, of the betting baize and clearly view the signals given by the tracker.

It is possible for one person to render the prediction and place the bets. It is not easy, but it is the way I prefer to play. If you are able to perform this feat, then you will eliminate the need for signals and save yourself an extra second or so of valuable betting time. In this event, you must gain a position next to the wheel, or maybe one person over. I refer to this as the first-base position. You will need to see the wheel and reach the layout. The person doing the betting should organize his chips into like piles with the same number of chips. I find that usually five or ten $1 chips per pile works best on a $5 or $10 minimum table. You will grab one pile and cover five numbers (one each for $5 and two each for $10) after you make your prediction. As your skill increases, you can advance up to $5 and even $25 chips. Black ($100) action inside draws too much heat!

Whether working alone or with a companion, the tracker jumps into action as soon as the ball is released. The tracker will time the rotor revolution for consistency. After observing the same wheel speed index number he saw on previous spins, he proceeds to continue with his tracking. On subsequent spins, he will continue to time the rotor right after the ball is released to ensure that this index number has not changed. Now that he has observed a constant wheel speed, he will study the intersections or alignments between the ball and the rotor. He will focus on the single and double zeroes as he waits for the 2-X crossover pattern to appear. Always being aware of where the zeroes are relative to some pre-selected stationary point in the bowl at any given time.

The tracker knows that to best observe the 2-X crossover, he should select a third of the bowl to view the pattern. This third of the bowl is situated just CCW of the anticipated drop-off point and will contain one 120-degree set of intersecting vectors that form the 2-X crossover at T– 4 ball revolutions. A point of observation such as a vertical deflector, within this one-third bowl, will be used to gauge a rotor number (our observation number) that can later be correlated to the final number. This same stationary point, or deflector, may have been used earlier to index the wheel speed. The tracker follows both the single-zero and double-zero numbers as they enter his third of the bowl, keeping an extra eye on the ball as it races by in the upper track. Following the intersection points of the ball with the 0 and 00 he notices that the ball is slightly faster than twice the rotor speed. As the alignment formation tightens up, our player knows that the 2-X crossover is imminent.

For this particular wheel speed, let us assume that the ball drops when it slows to a speed equal to that of the rotor (the 1-X crossover pattern will occur). Each situation will be a little different depending upon the velocity of the rotor. The tracker is starting to get familiar with the pattern formations after observing previous spins for this particular wheel, at this wheel speed. The 2-X crossover is visible now, so he knows the ball is four revolutions away from dropping off the upper track. Our tracker has a consistent point in the event to take a reading (T – 4 ball revolutions before drop off). He now knows when the ball will break. He has created an octant drop histogram so he knows from where the ball will likely break.

Taking a snapshot at this point in time, the number 10 lines up with the stationary observation point at T – 4 ball revolutions. From previous trials, our tracker knows that the observation number at T – 4 revolutions is situated about 180 degrees away from the pocket number that will be directly under the ball when it drops. Perhaps the number 28 or 9 will be there when the ball breaks from the upper race. The tracker will have to observe this and possibly recalibrate his prediction on subsequent spins.

Let's say that the ball breaks and the number 9 is under it. The ball spirals down and crosses onto the rotor a quarter of the bowl later. Well, at the same time that the ball circled one-quarter revolution, the rotor will have also rotated one-quarter turn (remember that the ball and rotor are traveling at the same speed during the ball-drop for this example). Effectively, the ball strikes the rotor one-quarter + one-quarter (= one-half) of the wheel away, near the 25. It just so happens that the 10, just one pocket CCW of the 25, was our observation number back at T – 4 ball revolutions. The tracker has determined that the average ball bounce is about nine pockets, or one-quarter of the wheel. (You may want to create a ball-bounce histogram to determine this.) He adds nine more pockets to where the ball first entered the rotor at 25, and voila!, he has his prediction of 6! The tracker will correlate the observation number, 10, to the strike number of 25 by subtracting one pocket (going CCW). He will add on the nine pockets allotted for bounce in the clockwise direction.

Hence, back at T – 4 ball revolutions, the wheel tracker knew that his observation number was one pocket CCW from his rotor strike number. He simply added eight pockets (the average number of bounce pockets attributed to that wheel/ball combination minus the CCW adjustment to the strike number) to the T – 4 observation number of 10 and formed a prediction of 6. Because our tracker has the wheel thoroughly memorized, he instantly knows that on either side of the 6 are 18 and 21 (looking at the numbered rotor). And, on either side of the 18 and 21, are 31 and 33, respectively.

The tracker now has to get the money out on the betting layout. He has maybe two or three seconds to cover the numbers 6, 18, 21, 31 and 33 with his roulette chips, probably in that order, or reversed. This depends on which end of the layout he starts pelting with chips. So now he has covered a five-number sector centered about the predicted number 6. This all accomplished before that familiar cry of "No-o more bets!" Piece of cake . . . right?

Biased-Wheel Play

The basic idea behind biased-wheel play is to find a roulette wheel that produces a higher frequency of certain individual numbers, or certain sectors of numbers on the rotor, and then bet on those numbers. Some authors would simply have you look up at the tote board, pick the hot number, and bet on it. Chances are you will just be killing a couple of hours and a C-note, but who knows? You will not do worse than the random players will and depending upon whether a wheel or dealer bias does exist, you may actually find a hot number to ride.

However, for those of you who are more serious about biased-wheel play, you will want to locate a wheel bias that is *statistically significant*. Whole books have been dedicated to finding biased wheels. One such worthwhile book is Russell Barnhart's *Beating the Wheel: Winning Strategies at Roulette*. The book uses mathematics to support the concepts presented; however, it still reads more like a novel than a textbook. Many interesting real-life accounts are described in this 216-page biased-wheel handbook. Another great source of information for the serious biased-wheel player is a self-published nine-page report by Laurance Scott, simply titled, "Biased Wheel Report." Do not let the size fool you. It is a power pack full of serious let's-get-down-to-business material.

A biased wheel will favor one or more numbers due to some physical defect either formed over a long life of wear and tear with substandard maintenance (not too common), or during the manufacturing process (rarer still). Older wheels are more prone to biases because they have been in service longer and/or were manufactured with less than perfect technology. These older-style wheels were manufactured with individual frets or pocket separators that had to be individually positioned and fixed into place around the rotor. As a result, some pockets might be a little larger than other ones, thus giving them a better chance of capturing the ball. In addition, these frets tend to loosen over time. A loose fret absorbs more of the ball's energy, bringing it to a stop sooner. The older wheels also had wooden pocket bottoms that were painted with a resilient red, black or green paint. When the paint in certain pocket bottoms wore thin, the much softer wood underneath absorbed the ball's energy and lessened the bounce. These biases found on older wheels will cause a particular pocket to be favored. Unfortunately, the wheels manufactured today have one continuous ring of precision cast pockets, eliminating these potential reasons for biases.

An Early Biased-Wheel Player

In his book *Beating the Wheel: Winning Strategies at Roulette*, Russell Barnhart wrote about an English engineer who won because of his cleverness and not his good luck. By 1873, the Monte Carlo Casino saw its share of big winners and big losers. They were usually royalty or successful merchants with money to stake, and they either had good luck or bad luck. But in the long run all them found themselves in the red as roulette is a negative-expectation game when luck is your strategy.

Francois Blanc, who ran this magnificent casino, understood the nature of luck, that wild winning and losing streaks were par for the course, but that eventually the house would win. Thus, Blanc was not too worried when someone became overly fortunate. He knew that his establishment possessed the mathematical edge over the long term and that the pendulum would swing back to the house's favor in time.

However, Blanc and his casino were not ready for one Joseph Jaggers, at least not right away. Jaggers was an English engineer and mechanic who became fascinated with the roulette wheel itself. These instruments were supposed to be delicately balanced mechanisms producing purely random results, but Jaggers doubted their accuracy. He hired six clerks to sit down at each of six roulette tables and write down the results as they appeared. This activity of wheel clocking was not illegal, nor uncommon at the tables. At the end of one week of recording, Jaggers had about 3,000 spins on each of six wheels. That was all the ammunition he needed.

One of the six wheels was sufficiently biased to cause him great excitement and he decided to put his money where his math was. The engineer began betting on nine individual numbers, six of which were contained in one sector. By the time he was ahead some 50,000 francs ($10,000), he had two worried inspectors watching him. By the time he had amassed 250,000 francs three inspectors were trying to figure out what system he was employing. They wondered if he was somehow cheating. At the end of the night, the Yorkshire engineer was up an incredible 350,000 francs. That translated into about $70,000 at the time.

Jaggers was worried that the casino might figure out what he was up to so he began to arbitrarily add other numbers in the mix, hoping to throw them off the scent. It worked well. Four days later, the casino had lost an astounding 1.5 million francs to Jaggers alone! It seems that scores of onlookers began to cap Jaggers' bets with bets of their own. A desperate casino manager finally realized that Jaggers always played the same roulette wheel. He figured it must be unbalanced in some way so he had all the roulette wheels shuffled to different tables after closing.

When an unsuspecting Jaggers sat down to play the next day, he gave back a huge one million francs before realizing that the wheel he was playing looked slightly different. He recalled a slight scratch on the bowl of the original wheel and he ceased wagering. After carefully checking the other tables, he found the biased wheel and resumed betting. Jaggers was able to win back the one million francs he had lost earlier, plus an additional 750,000 francs for good measure. This brought his total up to an incredible 2.25 million francs or about $450,000!

Meanwhile, the manufacturers of the wheels were summoned to solve the problem. They correctly assumed some sort of bias and created movable frets. These frets could be adjusted or removed at any time as needed. The new frets were couriered over to the casino and fitted onto the six wheels. After subsequently losing 375,000 francs, Jaggers figured the casino had sufficiently foiled his efforts and bid farewell to the Monte Carlo. At the time Jaggers decided to call it quits, he was up a staggering 1,625,000 francs or $325,000. He never returned to Monte Carlo.

Modern Wheels

Because most major casinos use modern wheels, it is unlikely that you will ever find a pocket-biased wheel. Nevertheless, modern wheels may still be susceptible to biased sectors (groups of adjacent pockets on the rotor). Many different defects, or combinations of defects, could cause biased-wheel sectors, such as a slightly bent central spindle, a warped wheel head, an unevenly worn ball track, a tilted wheel, balls that are not perfectly round or balanced and so on. Also, the conditions that cause biases to appear may only occur at certain temperatures, times of day, or only for a certain range of rotor speeds, making them dealer dependant. It can get very cumbersome trying to keep track of all the potential variables that may influence the data and the conditions surrounding these variables.

I used the term statistically significant earlier, so let me address the frequency of a number's outcome and what it means to the biased-wheel player. There are 38 numbered pockets on an American roulette wheel. If totally left to chance, the probability of any number coming up on the next spin is 1/38 and if it were a fair game, you would be paid 37 to 1. But, in fact, you are paid as if there were 36 numbers on the wheel (winning 35 to 1). Therefore, any single-number bias that you decide to play must average at least one win every 35.5 spins (lose 69 units, win 70 units to net +1 unit). Otherwise, you will not have a positive expectancy.

The lower the number of spins it takes on average to produce a biased number, the higher the frequency of its occurrence, that is, the more often it comes up. The higher its frequency of occurrence, the stronger the bias will be—and the stronger that bias, the better! A number that hits once every 32 spins (lose 31 units, win 35 units to net +4 units) is over eight times more profitable than our one hit in 35.5 trials (71 spins to win 1 unit versus 64 spins to win 8 units). If you locate a wheel that produces a particular number once every

35.5 trials, you will have a positive edge. However, each reduction in the number of trials (on average) that it takes to produce the biased number is very meaningful indeed!

The Normal Distribution

We must observe the wheel for an appropriate length of time and record the results. These results or outcomes are our sample space. The larger the number of samples, "n," that we have obtained, the more confident we are that our results are representative of the real situation. We can measure the bias and gain confidence by using some elementary statistics. Now is a good time to discuss the concept of the normal curve.

The normal distribution, or the bounded area under the normal curve and above the y-axis, describes countless sets of data in nature, industry and research. It can be used to describe a series of outcomes one would observe from a random roulette wheel. The normal curve is shown in **Diagram 4-A**. We will compare our observed data with the data set under the normal curve to see if it is truly biased and to what extent.

The normal distribution is a continuous probability distribution, and the outcomes from a series of roulette trials are actually a discrete binomial distribution. We can, however, accurately approximate a discrete binomial distribution with a continuous normal distribution if "n" (the number of recorded trials) is very large and "p" (the probability of an event's success) is not extremely close to either zero or one (0 percent or 100 percent). If "p" is reasonably close to 1/2 (which is ideal), then "n" need not be as large to develop a very good approximation of just how biased the results are. This is why, when using a normal distribution to confirm a single-biased pocket (probability of 1/38), a lot more trials are required than when validating a 19-pocket sector with a probability of 19/38 or 1/2. The probability of hitting our sector is simply the number of pockets in the sector divided by 38 total pockets for an American wheel or 37 pockets for a French wheel, whichever the case may be.

The closer our probability is to 50 percent, the smaller the number of trials needed to gain an accurate understanding of the situation. You know that "p" represents the probability that a particular event will occur. You also know that "n" represents the number of trials in our sample space. You now know that we will need to compare our observed sample data with the area, or distribution of random data under a normal curve, sometimes referred to as a bell-shaped curve. If our frequency of occurrence for a select number(s) is higher than expected for a random roulette wheel over a significant number of trials, then we have a nonrandom or biased wheel.

The mean, or expected value of a randomly based distribution is of special importance. It not only describes the expected average of occurrence, but it also defines where the normal probability distribution is centered. For example, if we looked at the expected frequency of, say, the number 5 over 380 spins, we would expect ten occurrences, or one hit every 38 trials. Ten is the expected average, or mean, for a single number resulting on a random wheel spun 380 times. Our bell-shaped curve will find its vertical axis of symmetry centered at our calculated mean of ten. The recorded number of 5s will probably be higher or lower on a random wheel for such a small number of trials, but its average will begin to converge on the expected average of 1 in 38 as you collect more and more data. For a random wheel, the chances that we will be closer to the expected mean after 3,800 spins is far greater than it would be for just 380 spins. The same goes for 38,000 trials versus 3,800 trials.

Chances are we may never land on the exact mean or expected average, but we will get proportionally closer to this average as we record more spins—that is, unless the wheel truly is biased. Then we will converge on some other average that reflects the biased situation. The trick is to determine whether we have discovered a biased mean, or if we have just not converged on the random one yet. If it appears that we are beginning to converge on a biased average for our recorded data, we will need some level of confidence to know that it is truly biased and not just some statistical fluctuation. We will need to calculate how much our data deviates from the expected mean and that means it is time to discuss the concept of standard deviation, denoted by "s."

Standard Deviation

Without getting too technical, standard deviation helps us to determine how far we are from the expected mean, and what the chances are that our data is based solely on luck as opposed to being genuinely biased. One standard deviation is calculated as follows: s = sqrt (npq), where the standard deviation is equal to the square root of the number of trials times the random probability of winning multiplied by the random probability of losing (which is $1 - p$).

Let's say that we are tracking a single number. The probability of winning is $1/38$ so the probability of losing must be $1 - (1/38)$ or $37/38$. We happened to record 1,444 trials. So s = sqrt [1444 x (1/38) x (37/38)] or simply the square root of 37, which is 6.083. Our expected average is 1,444 times the probability of winning, $1/38$. Hence, our expected mean, or average is 38 (I picked 1,444 trials because it works out nicer). For any normal distribution, 68.26 percent of the data under the curve is contained between the (mean − 1s and mean + 1s) range.

For our example above, 38 is the mean and our standard deviation is about six. That means there is about a 68.3 percent chance that, after recording any arbitrary number on the wheel for 1,444 spins, our count will be in the range of 32 to 44 hits with an expected average of 38. There is a 15.87 percent chance of hitting more than 44 times, and because of symmetry about the mean, an equal 15.87 percent chance of hitting fewer than 32 times (15.87 percent + 68.26 percent + 15.87 percent = 100 percent). So after recording 1,444 spins, we find that our number hits 45 times, there is an 84.13 percent chance that it is biased and a 15.87 percent chance that it is a fluctuation. If we would like more confidence, then we could go out two standard deviations. The chance of being between (mean – 2s and mean + 2s), or (38 – 12 and 38 + 12) is 95.46 percent. There is a 2.27 percent chance that the frequency of hits will be less than 26, and an equal chance of being greater than 50 (2.27 percent + 95.46 percent + 2.27 percent = 100 percent). Therefore, if our number has hit 51 times in 1,444 trials, there is only a 2.27 percent chance of it being due to luck. Here is where I would bet serious money!

If our number is only one standard deviation away from the mean, then we will need to collect more data. It may be biased, but we are not as sure. Therefore, we record anoth-

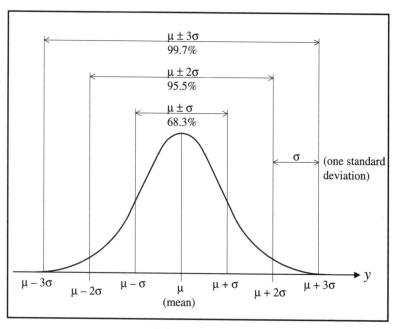

Diagram 4-A
The Normal Curve

er 1,444 trials for a total of 2,888. We calculate s = sqrt [2888 x (1/38) x (37/38)] or 8.60. Two standard deviations would be 17.2, or about 17. Our expected average is 76 hits in 2,888 spins. If we record 94 or more hits in 2,888 trials, there is better than a 97.73 percent chance of a bias.

By the way, as you accumulate data to check out a particular number, you may discover that the numbers adjacent to your suspected number may also be biased (a biased sector). Calculating the standard deviation for a sector is similar, only the probabilities change. As demonstrated earlier, the closer our probability of success is to 50 percent, the fewer the number of trials it will take to confirm the bias. Let us imagine that we suspect a five-pocket sector of being biased. Our probability of winning is 5/38 and our probability of losing is 33/38. We have observed the same 2,888 spins and recorded 420 hits on these five numbers. Where do we stand? Well, the average number of hits should be 2,888 spins times 5/38, or 380. Our 420 hits is well above the mean of 380. So, we are off to a good start.

Next, we calculate our break-even point. That is the number of trials multiplied the sector length, all divided by 36. Our break-even is 2,888 spins times 5/36, or slightly over 401 hits. We passed the second test. We are better than break-even. Now we need to test the deviance. I would recommend being two standard deviations above the mean: 2s = 2 x sqrt[2888 x (5/38) x (33/38)] or 2 x sqrt (330); 2s = 36.33. We would need 380 + 36.33, or better than 416 hits to confirm our bias. Any number of wins over 416 has better than a 97.73 percent chance of being biased. Our 420 hits passes this third test of deviance with excellence and comes in with a 98+ percent confidence rating.

More often, you will have to record additional spins to thoroughly confirm a bias. After performing many calculations and consulting with several experts, I have come up with some general rules of thumb for the number of recorded trials that you will likely need. If you are looking at a single-pocket bias, then record 10,000 spins. If you can show two standard deviations over the mean, you are in good shape. If it looks questionable, record another 5,000 spins and reevaluate. For a five-pocket sector, about 4,300 spins should confirm whether a bias is present or not. A nine-pocket sector will require about 2,000 trials to confirm its bias. That is why a team of wheel clockers is usually employed to gather all the preliminary data. Now imagine doing the above trials for 100 wheels to find the one that is biased and you now have a good idea of what is involved in attempting biased-wheel play.

One quick note, most casinos are aware of this potential weakness. Some casinos monitor their roulette wheels continuously for any bias. The results are constantly fed into on-line computers and thoroughly analyzed. Other, less sophisticated casinos will occasionally take a sampling of up to 10,000 spins and evaluate them for any bias. Even if they have no regular means of checking for biases, be careful not to tip them off. If you are camped out hour after hour, day after day, writing down results from all the roulette wheels, the casino may figure out what you are up to and thwart any chance to implement your scheme by simply readjusting the wheels.

Observing Two Biased-Wheel Players

Although I have never played a biased wheel, I did observe a middle-aged couple at work in the temporary Windsor Casino. He was tall, trim and nicely dressed. She was a leggy woman, a bit more casual, wearing shorts and her hair was clipped up in a bun. The couple worked in shifts, betting on numbers 33 and 35, just four pockets apart. I watched the gentleman placing his bets. He was putting $10 straight up on each of the two numbers. After witnessing a hit on number 35, I gathered up enough courage to approach him.

As he accepted his winnings in a businesslike manner, I commented, "Looks like you're having good luck with those numbers."

"Yeah, they're my kids' birthdays; they seem to be bringing me good luck right now," he said, not making eye contact with me.

As I retreated, another patron offered, "Either he or his companion have been playing those same numbers since last night . . . and doing very well at it." Maybe he's just lucky, I thought as I headed home for the day.

The next day I made my way back to the casino. There he was at the same table, playing those same numbers. I looked more closely—he was now wagering $50 units on each number! Now he had my full attention. After about 20 minutes, his female friend came over to relieve him. Just on her third spin she hit straight up on the number 35 for $1750.

"Wow! That's a beautiful hit. Do you always play those numbers?"

Not quite as composed as her male counterpart, she replied, "Oh, . . . uh yeah. My birthday and my anniversary date."

"Do you know the gentleman who was here earlier?" I asked. "He was playing the same numbers. He said he was playing his kids' birthdays, 3-3 and 3-5."

She looked at me for a second. "Sometimes," she conceded, in a softer tone, "certain numbers come up more often than they should. Now I must get back to business."

I came back a few days later, but they were gone. I asked the dealer at the table if he saw the couple in action. "I heard about some tall couple from one of the bosses," he said. "They played the same numbers and won over $12,000. After maintenance shuffled the wheels around, they disappeared."

I excitedly began charting the results of all twelve wheels over the next week, but I could not locate the wheel that produced all of those 33s and 35s. That was my brief brush with biased-wheel play.

Target Sectoring

Another interesting and innovative approach that I am including with the professional systems is called *target sectoring*. This method was first outlined and patented by Scott Lang, a mechanical engineer from Massachusetts. I personally do not know of anyone who was able to make money with target sectoring, but the concepts are based on elementary laws of physics and are valid. So, I am including target sectoring to help the reader gain a more rounded understanding of the game. This approach could possibly work under the right set of circumstances, but first I will explain just what target sectoring is.

In his self-published book, *Beat Roulette with a New Patented Discovery,* Scott Lang states that there is a unique relationship where the timing of the velocity of the ball as compared to that of the rotor, allows one to predict in which sector of the wheel that the ball is likely to come to rest. You will recall that wheel tracking also depends heavily on this concept of ball-to-wheel relative timing. Before publishing his technique, Lang purchased his own B.C. Wills, 32-inch regulation wheel to test his hypothesis.

Target sectoring evolved from an aspect of the game of shuffleboard. In shuffleboard, a puck is thrust across a surface and onto a marked target area. If the puck is aimed and propelled with the appropriate amount of force, it will stop on the more coveted target area with the highest points awarded. To imagine this, in your mind, draw two lines that cross the path of the sliding puck. The first (designated as Line A) can be drawn a foot or so beyond the starting line. The second line (Line B) will be marked a few feet beyond Line A. The exact position of the lines are not critical, only that they remain fixed for the set of trials that we are observing and are between the starting point and ending point of the puck. As the puck is propelled from the starting line, it will eventually cross Line A and then Line B before approaching the target area. If an observer could measure the time it takes for the puck to travel from Line A to Line B with a digital stopwatch, he could project whether the puck will fall short of reaching the highest value target area, overshoot this area or land perfectly on it, (assuming that no other pucks are in play).

Think about it. If the time interval from Line A to Line B is small, then the puck is traveling very fast. The faster the puck, the better the chances of overshooting the entire target area. Conversely, the longer the measured time from A to B, the slower that the puck is moving. It may never even reach the target area. The key to this whole concept is simple. If our playing conditions remain the same, there is an optimal and consistent time period that will predict a perfect thrust of the puck for the high-value target area. Furthermore, for any measured increment of time between lines A and B, there exists a projected point where the puck will stop. This is because the measured time directly correlates to an initial thrust velocity applied to the puck. This initial thrust velocity dictates the distance that the puck will travel before all of its energy is expended.

Likewise the ball, which represents the puck, is propelled in the upper track. When its energy is completely spent, it will come to rest in one of the numbered pockets. Lang first tested his hypothesis on his roulette wheel while the rotor was stationery. If he could show a consistent pattern of timings, he was half way home. Within several hundred spins, he was able to define a table of ball-to-wheel timings that correlated well to a predicted number or sector. The results fell into a well-defined table of timings for this one wheel with a constant rotor speed of zero degrees per second (or standing still).

The actual game of roulette is more complicated, but the same laws apply. For casino roulette, we must measure our time interval against a constantly spinning rotor (opposite direction) and compare relative speeds. Not only is our target moving, but it is cycling or repeating. Because of the wide range of wheel speeds possible, Lang had to record over 30,000 spins with the wheel head rotating, in order to statistically confirm his hypothesis.

Ball-to-Wheel Timing (Relative Velocity)

We can pick one reference point, say the single 0, and time the period from where the ball aligns with it on one revolution to an alignment on a successive revolution. This time will clue us into where the ball will break, strike the rotor, and finally come to rest. You will click on the stopwatch as it aligns with the zero (your first pass for timing purposes) and then stop the watch on the third intersection or alignment with the zero. Lang recommends waiting "some" number of ball revolutions to time the ball against the rotor in a particular range of ball speeds. The appropriate moment to time the ball against the rotor can be learned through experience and judgment according to Lang. The player will attempt to time the relative positions when the ball-to-wheel timing is in the 1.5 to 2.5 seconds range. I believe this may be possible for someone with keen eyesight and an impeccable sense of timing, but that would be the exception, not the norm.

There is a wide range of ball speeds that can be measured from any one intersection of the single zero to the third. To make the problem manageable, you must be able to select the same, or close to the same, set of intersection points (or ball revolutions) before the ball drops off. Scott Lang recommends waiting "some" number of ball revolutions before timing the first to third pass that the ball makes with the single zero. If the croupier launches the ball with much velocity, you will wait longer, until the ball slows sufficiently (using your judgment) to a point where it is in your range of recorded speeds. This is similar to Laurence Scott using crossover patterns to identify a specific T – n ball revolution to base his predictions on in wheel tracking. In fact, I would highly recommend using the crossover patterns while employing target sectoring as well. Why guess when you can identify an exact T – n ball revolution to time? Otherwise, you might very well time the wrong revolution. In that case, you will have to abort the prediction or rely on a wider range of ball-to-wheel timing charts with which to compare data. To compile a wide range of timing charts, you, like Scott Lang, would have to record some 30,000 trials for that specific wheel! So, learn how to spot and use the crossover patterns.

A Problem with Different Rotor Speeds

There are two key ways to greatly reduce this problem down to a more practical level. These are not discussed in Lang's book. The first was already mentioned, to learn and use the crossover patterns to identify a specific ball revolution for timing. I think that Lang did not know about the crossover patterns. However, after years of experience, he was able to judge the proper ball speeds for timing through pure observation.

The second key is to only play one tight band of wheel-speed index numbers. You will collect data for one specific wheel speed and record timings at the T – n ball revolution. So, we consequently borrow a second concept from the wheel tracker's tool box: indexing the wheel speed for consistency.

If you select a rotor that is spinning at a constant velocity from trial to trial and are able to pick out an exact T – n ball revolution to time, then 200 to 300 spins should give you enough data to form your timing chart. This chart will only work for that one wheel speed. Referring back to the shuffle board example, changing rotor speeds is analogous to shifting observation Lines A and B around before taking timings. You cannot compare timings taken from one set of observation lines to predict the outcome of an entirely different set of observation lines.

If you are in a casino that you frequent often, index the rotor speeds to see which ones are more common. Select the most common speed and create your timing chart. Write down the name and a description of the dealer. Wheel speeds are usually dealer dependant. If a new dealer (or the present one for that matter) starts spinning the rotor with a different rotor velocity, then stop recording the ball-to-wheel times for that chart. Index the new wheel speed and start a fresh chart, or take a break. Ball-to-wheel times for different rotor speeds yield different results.

I am not sure if Lang realized that a constant angular wheel velocity is critical for his method to work, since he did not mention it. In fact, he published one universal chart that, I suspect, he believed would work for all rotor speeds. The problem with this assumption is simple. The same relative ball-to-wheel time for rotors spinning at a different speeds will point to a different moment in the spin's history.

For example, on the first trial, you record a ball-to-wheel time of two seconds. Let's say that the 1-X crossover pattern occurred, and your rotor speed was 0.5 revolutions per second in the CCW direction, while the ball speed was 0.5 revolutions per second in the CW direction. You see the pattern forming, so you get ready. They align and you start your timing. One second later, both the ball and wheel have traveled 0.5 revolutions and intersect again, 180 degrees away. One more second goes by (and another half revolution) and the ball and wheel align for the third time. At this point, you stop your watch and see that 200 hundredths, or 2.00 seconds, have elapsed. That is your ball-to-wheel relative velocity time. At this slow speed, the ball is very close to reaching the exit velocity from the upper track (if it hasn't already done so) and spiraling down to the rotor. This event is near its end. You are taking a snapshot of the situation, late in the spin's history. The ball and wheel may possibly cover one more revolution, then the result is determined.

On the next spin, the wheel head is sufficiently slowed down. It is now traveling at 0.333 revolutions per second. If you look for the same ball-to-wheel timing of 2.00 seconds, it will now occur at the 2-X crossover pattern. The ball would be spinning at 0.666 revolutions per second at this time (twice the speed of the wheel) and your ball-to-wheel time would still be 2.00 seconds! The ball may spin another four to six revolutions before exiting the upper track and striking the rotor. You are taking a snapshot much earlier in the history of that spin. It would be several revolutions out of sync with the first 1-X crossover example. While it is true that the additional distance covered by the faster spinning ball is partially compensated for by a more slowly rotating wheel head (opposite direction), the wheel will not perfectly offset the angular distance covered by the spinning ball. The ball decelerates much faster than the wheel does, hence the resultant sectors will shift to some unknown extent.

Remember that the velocity relationship is nonlinear. The amount of error incurred when using timings generated for a wheel speed of 0.5 revolutions per second to make predictions for a 0.333 revolutions per second wheel is much too large. You will have to create a new set of ball-to-wheel timings based on the 0.333 revolutions per second rotor. You might get away with a small amount of wheel speed error; perhaps one or two pockets off the index number, but no more. Personally, I would only deal with exact wheel speeds.

Other Dilemmas with Target Sectoring

Not only is target sectoring dependant upon constant angular wheel velocities, but it is sensitive to tilted or otherwise defective wheels. Anything that could alter the exit velocity from one spin to the next would cause difficulties. Tilted wheels may not work because the ball is forced to exit at a more consistent location than at a consistent exit velocity. If the ball exits the upper track at slightly different velocities due to tilt, then the timings will be slightly off.

The magnitude of error in your prediction is dependant upon the amount of tilt present. Ideally, you would want a perfectly level wheel for this method to work. Therefore, before you generate your timing chart, create an octant drop histogram to check for tilt. If the wheel is tilted such that 40 percent or more of the ball drops occur from one octant, then use the wheel tracking technique to take advantage of this situation. If the ball drops are spread out evenly, with less than 20 percent occurring at any one octant, then target sectoring might work. After awhile, you will become proficient at checking the wheel speed index, noticing the 2-X crossover pattern, taking the ball-to-wheel velocity time, remembering the octant drop and recording the final number, all for one spin!

There are several variables in the game of roulette that will give cause for generating multiple-timing charts. As already discussed, different dealers with different wheel speeds create variable timing situations. In addition, tilted or defective wheels will bias the fall-off position of the ball. A consistent ball drop is great for wheel tracking, but throws the timing slightly off for sector targeting. Different wheels will more than likely require different sets of timing charts. Features, such as the gradual escape upper track versus the older style ledge, will affect when and how the ball will spiral down to the rotor. High fret designs versus low frets, or continuous fret rings, will all affect the ball bounce to a great extent. A high fret design may only allow four or five pockets of bounce, while a continuous fret design could easily see 38 pockets or more skip by.

Even if everything else is exactly the same, any amount of ball bounce variance will require different timing charts. The size and style of ball deflectors can affect the timings. Smaller deflectors may have a negligible effect on altering the ball's final approach. This is better for all methods of play. Aside from working with different wheels and different dealers, different balls will also yield unique results. The size, material and method of manufacture will cause different balls to react differently enough to alter the timing. Watch carefully to ensure that the balls are not being switched. If a dealer alternates balls while you are attempting to create a chart, you will have to keep multiple charts to account for this. This method is dependant upon which particular ball is in play.

While I find target sectoring intriguing, it requires ideal circumstances. Target sectoring relies solely on precision timing and may be too sensitive to real world conditions. Anything that alters the ball's exit velocity a few hundredths of a second will throw off the timing. In addition, the amount of human error involved while taking the timing may be too high. My experiences tell me that most people cannot differentiate properly between one-tenth of a second when following the little white ball, let alone a few hundredths.

Then there are the many variables that might warrant having to create whole new sets of timing charts altogether. Four different wheel speeds, with three different dealers and two different balls could easily require 24 different timing charts for the same wheel! Then multiply that by six or eight different wheels in one casino and the possibilities become overwhelming.

References for Professional Play

Here are three publications that will advance your general roulette studies:

1. *The Mathematics of Gambling* by Dr. Edward O. Thorp, Lyle Stuart

2. *The Eudaemonic Pie* by Thomas A. Bass, Penguin Books

3. *Roulette Wheel Study* by Ron Shelley, Self-Published

And if your thirst exceeds these books, then add the following three for specialized studies:

For finding and beating biased wheels:

Beating the Wheel: Winning Strategies at Roulette by Russell T. Barnhart, Lyle Stuart

For visual or wheel tracking techniques:

How to Beat Roulette, an Expert Level System for Clocking the Wheel by Laurance Scott, Self-Published

For target-sector timing techniques:

Beat Roulette with a New Patented Discovery by Scott Lang, Whirling Lady Press

In the next section we will tie everything up into a neat little bundle by giving you a more feasible methodology to use. This approach will take the physical phenomena into account, but will be more practical for the weekend or part-time player to employ.

Part 5

Predictive Systems for the Part-time Player

Dealer's Signature and Relative Numbers

"What are dealer's signatures and relative numbers?" you may be asking. "Do I get the dealer's autograph, then ask him for his great aunt's number?" Well, not quite. The dealer's signature refers to a certain tendency that a dealer will exhibit when spinning the rotor and then snapping the ball into play. It is believed that well-practiced dealers, spinning hour after hour for shift after shift develop an automatic and repetitive delivery. This *signature delivery* tends to foster results that are more predictable. The idea of dealers having signatures has been around for a good twenty years.

Stephen Kimmel wrote about it in his article titled "Roulette and Randomness" in the December 1979 issue of *Gambling Times*. The concept is a bit more complex than Stephen first realized, but his basic idea is valid—dealers do have signature deliveries and some of these dealers are in fact predictable to a greater or lesser extent. There are some key conditions that you will need to watch for when considering signature play. We will cover these later in this chapter.

A relative number is typically used to describe the number of pockets that a ball has landed on the present trial—relative to the resulting number on the previous trial. For example, the dealer hits a 15 on the first spin that you observe. On the next spin, a 25 is hit. The third spin produces a 4. So, we count along the wheel in the direction that the ball is thrown (clockwise). Starting at 15, we count nine pockets in the clockwise direction until we come upon 25. Next, we count 11 pockets from the 25 to the number 4. So far, it looks like the dealer is consistently hitting about ten pockets away from the previous number. If we choose to play this apparent signature, we would probably cover the number 11 (ten pockets away) along with the 7, 30, 20 and 26 on either side of the 11. If the 11 pocket were indeed hit, then 24 would be the next target on the following spin.

There are both proponents and opponents for this school of thought. Having firsthand experience, I believe that it is possible for dealers to develop patterns or signatures. Several years back, I rented a 32″ regulation wheel and had it set up in my dining room. With the camcorder rolling, I practiced spinning the ball with various rotor speeds and wheel tilts. After 24 total hours of practice, I realized that, with the right wheel speed and a consistent delivery, my results did not appear to be random. I became proficient at aiming for and hitting targeted areas and even specific numbers (at times) on the wheel. This ability seemed to phase in, get stronger and then start to phase out. Sometimes I could adjust the wheel speed slightly and maintain it a little longer. Wanting to show off my new talent, I volunteered to run the roulette game for any Vegas Night that would have me. As you can imagine, I was faced with a dilemma. Do I use my skill to spin against the patrons . . . or maybe help some of them out? I decided to be a company man for the most part. At one church that I worked for every year, they dubbed me "the cleaner." I could bring them in with a quick hit early on, then milk 'em slowly. I have had experiences over the past

few years that were interesting, amusing and unbelievable
. . . like the time a boss dared me (during a slow time) to hit
number 29. I had been practicing my skill at an empty table,
so I was zoned in. I kicked the wheel speed up, just slightly,
lined up the number in my sights, and snapped the ball the
same way I had been doing all night. The ball broke from the
upper track, with a short spiral down the apron, crossed onto
the rotor, and settled in the number 29 pocket! "No way you
can pull that one off again," he remarked.

I kicked the wheel up, launched the ball, and, you
guessed it, number 29! This time the boss was quiet. I picked
the ball up and for good measure gave it another go. With the
boss still looking on, I sniped out a third 29! That was three in
a row! "Stop showing off," he quipped, and went back about
his business. Now I have to admit, deep frets or not, this
should have been a 1 in 54,872 long shot if it were truly random!

Another experience involved a loud, obnoxious man
demanding a hit on one of his numbers. This guy was splitting the 13-14, 17-20, 16-19 and 32-33. He also was playing the
numbers 3 and 7 straight up. As a service to everyone present,
I decided to lose this loud, smoke-blowing, beer-guzzling
gambler in record time. He gave me two eleven-pocket sectors centered about the 0 and 00 to shoot for. None of his
numbers were near the zeroes. After avoiding his area for ten
or twelve straight trials, he only had five chips left to make his
bets. He quickly covered the splits and now had one chip left.
I could see him struggling with his decision as to covering the
3 or the 7. "Would you like to purchase another chip?" I
offered.

"No, no, no, uh, let me think," he blurted. Finally, he
bet his last chip on the 7.

"Wrong answer," I thought to myself.

"Are you sure?" I asked him. "Yeah, you just pick up
that little white ball and give it a twirl," he sniped.

"You're the boss," I said, as I kicked up the wheel speed and snapped the ball. About ten seconds later, a big groan was heard from the end of the table as the ball settled rather comfortably in the number 3 pocket.

"Son-of-a-#$&!@, I knew that &*%-%#@$ number 3 would come up!" and with that he was gone. He never knew what hit him. There are more stories then space will permit here, but realize that the dealer's signature is truly a powerful phenomenon. The astute roulette player will learn how to recognize and exploit it.

On my last visit to the annual Las Vegas Gaming Expo, usually held in October, I worked as an exhibitor for *casino.com*. I had the opportunity to speak with the Director of Gaming for a major casino located on one of the smaller Caribbean Islands. This soft spoken, well-dressed gentleman was accompanied by his assistant. He had dealt roulette for 14 years and was in management for an additional nine. After we talked a brief while, I asked him what he thought about dealer's signature. "Oh, yes indeed, there is something to it. Would you like see a demonstration?" he offered.

"Sure," I replied. This is great, I thought. This director with over 23 years experience is going to show me dealer's signature firsthand. He led me over to a booth with what looked like a Huxley Mark 5 wheel. The exhibitors seemed to know the director as he stepped behind a table and took control of the wheel.

After only two practice spins, he began to call out his target pocket before each ball snap. Wow, this guy is not only demonstrating signature, he is demonstrating ball control! With about half a dozen spins each, he proved proficiency at three different wheel speeds. The director was obviously anxious to show that he still had it. He was able to hit within two pockets of his target number and was never more than five pockets away! As a crowd began to gather, he showed different ball releases (some snaps were faster than any I had ever seen). I was initially eager to show off my dealing skills, but after witnessing his mastery of the game, I decided to contain myself. As far as he knew, I was a software programmer or something similar. After the demonstration, he told me that skilled croupiers were in demand and even received bonuses. He did not offer any further details, though.

Recognizing a Signature Phase-in

What are the signals that we look for when locating a signature? The first thing we need to observe is whether or not the dealer's results are creating some kind of pattern around the wheel. Once you understand how the numbered pockets are laid out on the wheel, you will begin to develop an idea of their relative positions to each other. In **Part 3**, I extensively covered the American- and French-style wheel layouts and some betting techniques for capitalizing on them. If, for example, you track a dealer who has hit a 21, then an 18, then a 6, you'll notice that the last three numbers hit within a three-pocket sector . . . not bad. This dealer is hitting the same area of the wheel. His average relative number is currently 38, which means that the ball is landing some multiple of 360 degrees away from its last resting spot. You may seriously consider using some of the techniques discussed previously for betting the red second dozens, or you can cover a five-numbered sector centered about the number 6 (in this case) with wheel chips if you have time. There are many betting options (review **Part 3** as needed).

The point I want to make here is that you need to develop the ability to see the resultant patterns. Often you will find a dealer who is hitting a quarter of the wheel away from the last outcome, or a third of the wheel, or any fraction you can think of. The key is consistency. You will have to determine what pattern (if any) that the dealer is falling into, how strong the pattern is, and what betting tactics you will employ.

Many casinos in this modern day have tote boards displayed. Use the tote board to initially bring yourself in for a closer look. Verify first that the tote board is working (they sometimes malfunction) and, secondly, that the current dealer was responsible for throwing the numbers that interested you. Many times a certain dealer will be scheduled for a particular table/wheel, but he will only work 40 minutes out of the hour. A relief dealer will come for the remaining 20 minutes until the regular dealer comes back.

Sometimes dealers will rotate tables, and other times relief dealers will float from table to table. Just ask someone who appears to be camped out at that table (someone who is seated and has a stack of the colored wheel chips) to verify the tote board's accuracy and the dealer's presence.

Another tip-off to a potentially good situation is finding dealers that you already know are consistent in their delivery. If you frequent a particular casino, you will begin to get familiar with these dealers' styles and habits. After observing just a few spins, you will know if their signature is working.

A couple of months back, I stopped in at the new Windsor Casino one evening. George, one of my favorite dealers, was practically stopping the ball on a dime. The last four numbers were 2, 0, 2 and 2. Not only are the 0 and 2 right next to each other on the wheel head, but they are also adjacent to each other on the betting baize as well (the only split bet that this is true for). I confirmed that George threw the last four numbers and that they were correct.

After the next spin (that same type of spin George has shown me hundreds of times before), I placed a $25 green chip for me and a $1 white one for him on the 0-2 split. George gave me a quick smile. "No more bets" he called out. The ball entered the rotor at the 16 pocket and took a series of short hops to its final resting place . . . the single zero!

"Very nice sir," George said as he pushed 17 quarters over to me. "Eighteen and down," he yelled over his shoulder to the pit (his $17 win plus the original $1 bet).

"Let's try one more, George," I said as I split the 0-2 with $26 again. I watched as the ball came down into the 21, but it exited the rear of the pocket and got hung up on the central cone. Wind resistance killed the ball's forward momentum and pushed it back to the 8 pocket. "Hey, George, it was fun. Maybe I'll catch you a little later," I remarked. He thanked me and I headed off for a break.

George's had been an obvious pattern to spot. Five spins in a two-pocket sector. Plus, I was familiar with George's delivery. If we take the first hit to establish the pattern, then calculate the probability of the next four results being in the same two-pocket sector, we would have a 1 in 130,321 chance of randomly witnessing such a feat. A consistent and propitious roulette dealer can be your best friend in the entire casino world.

Verifying the Dealer's Signature

This is the more technical part of this section. At this point, you are familiar with the dealer's signature. This refers to the tendencies that some dealers exhibit at certain times to produce patterns or a signature. Because you understand how the wheel head is laid out, you will recognize these patterns when you see them appear on the tote board. You now have several betting tactics that you can employ in different circumstances. You will look for a croupier who is caught in a particular area of the wheel head or is exhibiting a strong relative number pattern.

Dealers can phase in and out of a signature. You will have to be ever-watchful. They are human, and humans are creatures of habit, but they are also affected by their environment. So, as a result, the dealer will settle into a groove, but disruptions like extended payoffs, breaks, shifting to different tables, etc. can break up a smoothly running routine. Because of these and other factors, I cannot give you absolute mechanical ways to play (i.e., dealer hits three numbers in a five-pocket sector, so bet the farm!), but I can give you *indicators* that will help you confirm an actual signature. This bonafide signature will be based on specific physical elements.

Let us look for the presence of three important conditions in order to take advantage of a signature. If this is a true signature, then these conditions should be met:

1. The velocity of the rotor must be the same each time the ball is snapped.

Surprisingly, over 90 percent of the dealers that I have encountered automatically kick the wheel speed right back up to where it was on the previous ball snap. Usually they have to make a conscious effort to change it up. We do not need to calculate the rotor's angular velocity, but we do need a test that will show timing consistency from one trial to the next. Select a vertical deflector that is just in front of the dealer. After the dealer kicks the wheel speed back up (just before releasing the ball), watch for the single zero. As soon as it passes under your diamond deflector, begin your count or cadence. When complete, observe the number that is directly under your vertical deflector. That is your wheel speed index number. If this wheel speed index number is the same from trial to trial, then you have a croupier who rotates the wheel head at a constant angular velocity (the wheel speed is the same).

You may remember in the previous section on wheel tracking, that we discussed techniques for gauging the wheel speed. Review this portion of **Part 4** if you need to. Only play dealers who are spinning with the same rotor velocity (consistent wheel-speed index number). Assuming that your judgment will not be perfect from trial to trial, we will allow plus or minus one pocket error on the rotor timing. Make sure that you use the same cadence or song fragment on each occasion to time the rotor. Oh . . . and sing silently to yourself or you may find an audience listening!

2. The rotating ball should complete the same number of revolutions each time, before entering the rotor. The idea here is that the ball is snapped with the same initial velocity, which will cause it to make the same number of revolutions in the upper track before succumbing to gravity. From my experience, this condition is a little tougher to satisfy. If you were a wheel tracker, you would not worry about the ball's initial velocity. You would have to select the same ball revolution before it drops from the upper track, say T – 4 revolutions. At that consistent point, the ball's velocity will be the same from trial to trial. For dealer's signature play, we need a *consistent ball release*. After the dealer snaps the ball, count the number of revolutions that the ball travels in the upper track up to the time that it crosses onto the rotor. Use the eight ball deflectors to break the final revolution up into fractions. If, for illustrative purposes, the croupier spins the ball slightly to his right, aligning, perhaps, with a horizontal deflector, then you will use that reference point to gauge the number of passes that the ball makes. On the final revolution, it may pass that point and go, for example, three more deflectors before crossing onto the rotor. You would record or remember "11-3/8 ball revolutions."

We need a dealer who can throw the ball with at least plus or minus one-fourth of a revolution (19 total pockets). Our allowable error for ball revolutions, then, is plus or minus 9.5 pockets. For our example, 11-3/8 is the dealer's average ball revolutions per throw, so he will need to be in the 11-1/8 to 11-5/8 revolutions range. If the wheel is tilted, the tilt will help produce more consistent ball drops. On the last revolution, the ball will likely drop while it is climbing up the tilt to the apex. You can construct octant drop histograms for the wheels that you plan to play. This will give you added insurance for this second condition. In addition, ball deflectors come in different shapes and sizes. The smaller the diamond deflectors, the less risk of altering the ball's final approach as it spins down the apron to the rotor.

Remember, you will begin your revolutions count at the point of release and continue it until the ball crosses over the rim onto the rotor. With a little practice, this will become easy to do. A dealer's average can vary from session to session or wheel to wheel. You will have to evaluate his ball-revolutions average based on the consistency of his individual sessions. After several visits, you will compile a list of favorite or consistent dealers.

3. Once on the rotor, the ball's bounce must remain fairly constant from trial to trial. Determine the average ball bounce for the wheel/ball combination that you are playing. To do this, remember the pocket where the ball entered the rotor (at the instant you concluded your ball revolutions count) and compare it to the pocket where the ball finally comes to rest. This will tell you the number of pockets that the ball traveled once it crossed onto the rotor. Establish an average number of ball travel-pockets. In subsequent spins, we will allow plus or minus a six-pocket deviance for ball bounce. If your average ball bounce on the rotor is eight pockets, then you will accept a range of two to 14 pockets for ball travel on the rotor.

Here are some additional suggestions concerning ball bounce. Avoid playing against light roulette balls. Although standard in size, these balls are made of a lighter material. They are more easily affected by air resistance, path anomalies, such as varnish cracks and any foreign substances in the bowl, such as cigar ashes. Worst of all, they will react unpredictably when entering the spinning rotor. (Review **Part 3** for more details.) These balls are easy to spot. They look and act like ping-pong balls! Oftentimes they will get hung up on the outer rim of the rotor. Because these balls are lighter, the centrifugal force from the rotor pushes the ball radially out to the rotor's edge (away from the pockets). I have seen cases where the force of the ball's weight was not enough to subsequently pull it down into a pocket. As a result, the dealer had to call "no roll" and re-spin it. So it is very important to watch how the ball reacts when it enters the rotor. If you are in Atlantic City, watch the roulette balls at the Taj Mahal Casino. At the time of this writing, I noticed these balls react more like pith balls. Just avoid them altogether.

Another condition that will be detrimental to a signature is a swiftly rotating wheel head. The ball may absorb varying amounts of energy from the more massive rotor. Depending upon how the ball strikes the spinning rotor, it could end up in a number of different directions with a wide range of magnitudes because the reaction is too volatile. Avoid fast rotors. Something else to remember, although not as critical: higher frets (deeper pockets) will reduce ball bounce. If faced with the option, always select the older, deep-pocketed wheels. The more modern wheels today are designed with shallow pockets or low knife-edge frets. These induce a more volatile ball bounce.

An Important Point: *You will calculate relative numbers based upon the ball release point and not the last pocket number.* I know that we discussed relative numbers being based on a series of numbers that hit and their relationship to the prior numbers that hit. This common definition of relative numbers is fine most times for alerting yourself to a *potential* signature, but for *verification* purposes, I have had to tighten this definition up a little more. Typically, dealers will just snatch the ball out of the last pocket and release it right away, but sometimes they will release two pockets later on one spin and four pockets later, for example, on the next one. Worse yet, some dealers hold the ball out for a length of time before finally releasing it. If you base your relative-number judgment solely on the last pocket hit, then you will not account for any of these occurrences. Observe the number on the spinning rotor that is directly under the ball, the instant it is snapped. You will then compare this number to the final result to get your relative number for this spin.

Let us review this entire final section:

You approach a wheel that looks promising. The dealer kicks up the rotor speed just a little and snaps the ball. You instantly notice where the ball was snapped from in the bowl (probably right in front of the dealer) and what rotor number was directly under the ball when it was released. Using the same stationary reference point in the bowl, you chant your cadence, or song fragment, and note the wheel-speed index number. At the same time with your peripheral vision, you count the number of times that the ball has passed this stationary reference point. You continue to track the ball's revolutions until it breaks and enters the rotor or wheel head. At that point, you will estimate the ball's revolutions to the nearest deflector (or 1/8 of a revolution) and remember the rotor number where it entered the wheel head. The ball will bounce some number of pockets and come to rest. You immediately, and discretely, write on your scorecard:

1. The wheel speed index number.
2. The rotor release number.
3. The number of ball revolutions to the rotor.
4. The number of pockets traveled on the rotor.
5. The final resultant number.

Do not forget to write the dealer's name and a brief description at the top of the card. The release number and the final number will define the dealer's signature. The other data will help you confirm it. It will take a little practice to put this all together. Start by gauging the wheel speed and rotor release number. When you get comfortable with that, then keep adding one more task until you can master the whole procedure.

An alternate method would be to spot an apparent signature, then verify the wheel speed, ball revolutions to rotor and average ball bounce first and separately. Assuming that these conditions will remain constant, you simply note the rotor release number and add the relative number of pockets to this in the CW direction. Determine your target number and bet a sector centered about it. This second method is much easier to employ, but not quite as reliable.

Estimating the Error

Assuming a normally distributed sampling of errors, we can calculate the standard deviation of their combined effect on the signature. We will calculate the standard deviation, or "s" as the square root of the sum of the squares:

$$s = \text{sqrt} (\text{Error1}^2 + \text{Error2}^2 + \text{Error3}^2)$$

Where Error1 is the rotor timing error of plus or minus one pocket. Error2 is the ball revolution error of plus or minus 9.5 pockets and Error3 is the ball bounce error of plus or minus six pockets. Solving for "s" we get:

$$s = \text{sqrt} (1^2 + 9.5^2 + 6^2) = \text{sqrt} (127.25) = 11.28 \text{ pockets}$$

If we can contain the errors as described in the last section, then two-thirds (plus or minus one s) of the time, we will not be more than about 11 pockets off one way or the other. Another way to look at it, we have a target number (at the center of our sector) with a leeway of eleven pockets to the left, and eleven pockets to the right.

Suppose we bet one unit each on our 23-pocket sector (11 + 1 + 11) and we hit two-thirds of the time. Would we win or lose over the long haul? Let's do a break-even analysis. The number of pockets covered for a break-even situation is represented by "c." The number of units won will equal the number of units lost. We know that we will win two-thirds of the time, so we have the following scenarios:

1. We lose "c" units (no numbers hit), 1/3 of the time.

2. We win 35 units (on a straight up hit) and lose the other c – 1 units we wagered 2/3 of the time.

Because we break even, total units won – total units lost = 0, therefore:

$$2/3 \times [(35) - (c - 1)] - 1/3 \times (c) = 0;$$
$$\text{or } 70/3 - 2c/3 + 2/3 - c/3 = 0$$

$$72/3 - 2c/3 - c/3 = 0; \text{ or } 72/3 = 3c/3;$$
$$\text{or } c = 24.$$

Hence c, or the break-even sector length for a two-thirds win rate, is 24. You will lose 24 + 23 + 23 and win 35 + 35, which adds up to 0. Any sector less than 24 pockets in length that hits two-thirds of the time is a definite winner. Our 23-pocket sector is a definite winner if the error conditions can be met. One final point: you do not need to play all 23 numbers to take advantage of a signature. You will still enjoy your positive edge if you play only part of the 23-pocket sector, say, the five numbers in the center. Your win rate will be lower, but so too will your loss rate. As long as the resultant number is within plus or minus eleven pockets of your central target on the wheel head two-thirds of the time, you are playing with a positive advantage.

Practical Tips for Part-Timers

If you plan to play roulette only occasionally, the following information will help you prepare a maximum effort in a minimum timespan. You will seek tables where patterns of relative numbers are emerging. Then you will watch to see if the dealer has a consistent delivery style and keeps the wheel uniformly rotating. Depending upon the signature's strength, your bankroll and the situation in general, you will select a betting strategy and cautiously jump in. Many casinos have electronic tote boards mounted at the head of the table. The last 20 or so numbers that hit will be displayed. If you have an idea how the wheel head is laid out, you will recognize that certain patterns, or signatures appear from time to time.

One of the easiest patterns to spot is a dealer who is hammering the same area of the rotor. This is sometimes referred to as a *power sector*. If the dealer has hit a 17, 5, 22 and a 17 again, a power sector may be developing. Perhaps the dealer has hit a 7, 24, 12 and a 4. After inspecting the wheel diagram, you notice that the dealer is hitting nine pockets away from his previous number. He is exhibiting a strong nine pocket relative-number pattern. These are the two primary patterns, or signatures, that I want you to focus on playing.

One notable variation to these patterns involves a situation where a pocket 180 degrees away from the expected pocket results. You were anticipating a number near the single zero, for example, but for some reason a number closer to the double zero appears on the opposite side of the wheel. One of my associates, Eric Nielsen, has dubbed this the *180-degree phenomenon*. Sometimes the dealer will be hitting a certain sector on the wheel, but the third or fourth result ends up exactly one half of the wheel away. If you have played dealer's signature before and know your way around the rotor, then I'm sure that you have experienced what I am talking about. You will be playing what you thought was a 19-pocket relative-number pattern when the dealer starts hitting a power sector (relative number of 38).

Was his signature 38 or 19 pockets? You may be stumped at times. That is why you should consider playing opposing sectors when this happens. One way to do this is by betting the appropriate groups on the betting layout. In **Part 3** on sector slicing, we discussed how the black and red second-dozen numbers are directly across the wheel from each other. We also talked about how the third line (7 through 12), and ninth line (25 through 30), cover the six pockets immediately after the 0 and 00, 180 degrees away from each other. Refer back to this section for more examples.

Another way to bet opposing sectors on the American 00 wheel is to wager with split bets. You will recall that for every odd number on the double-zero wheel, the next higher number, an even number, is exactly 180 degrees away. Let us say, for example, that you liked the number 13, but the dealer was exhibiting the 180-degree phenomena on a frequent basis. You could cover two five-pocket sectors with only five chips. Simply split the zeroes, the 1-2, 13-14, 35-36 and the 23-24. You will notice that I listed the odd numbers first for each pair. That helps to keep the accounting easier. When I look at 13 and its two neighbors on each side, I see the 00. That is no problem; I will just split the zeroes at the very top of the layout. The 1 and 13 are next. I will cover these and the next highest numbers, 2 and 14. The 36 and 24 are even, so I will look for those numbers and the next lowest numbers on the layout.

Sometimes a bet calls for an odd number in the third column, such as the number 15. You will not be able to split the 15-16 because they are not next to each other. You have two choices here. If the 15 were at the center of your target sector or one pocket away, you would play it and the 16 straight up. If it is at the edge of your sector, you might consider leaving it naked, or not betting on it. A third option would be to play the 15 straight up and forget about the 16.

What causes the 180-degree effect? I am not exactly sure. It may be a combination of things. I remember one situation where the angular velocity of the ball at the point where it broke from the upper track was twice that of the slowly spinning rotor. The wheel was tilted, causing the ball to break from the same area of the upper track most times. A certain sector of the wheel was usually under the ball when it broke, but occasionally the ball broke one revolution sooner or later. In each case, the wheel head would be positioned 180 degrees out of phase. When this happened, there was a good chance that the ball would end up 180 degrees away. If I had not been comparing the ball's terminal velocity in the upper track to that of the wheel's constant angular velocity, I would not have known why this pattern was occurring.

Another instance where I noticed the 180-degree effect occurring was when the ball occasionally struck a vertical ball deflector. Most times, the ball just barely cleared this deflector, but once in awhile, it struck head on. When this happened, the ball was directed towards the rotor half a revolution earlier, and the ball settled in 180 degrees sooner. In both cases, the rotor was spinning at a consistent speed from trial to trial. There may be a dozen or more such situations where the mechanics dictate an occasional 180-degree hit. Do not worry so much about what causes the effect as much as how to properly play it.

You will also need to do some verifying work to help confirm the dealer's consistency. Are you comfortable with the number of results that make up the pattern? One result is not a trend and two hardly establish a pattern. I think three is the minimal number of outcomes that you will want to use if you spot a strong signature developing. For example, if I see a dealer who I know to be fairly consistent hit a 00, 27 and 1, then I might take a shot at playing the 13, 1, 00, 27 and 10 straight up. This covers a five-pocket sector centered about the tight formation of numbers he recently hit. If I win, I may continue to wager this area. If I lose, I will closely monitor this dealer to see if the pattern shifts, or manifests itself in some other form before I bet again.

There is no set number of results that will work every time for confirming a signature. If the formation is tight, and the dealer's routine is consistent, I may tiptoe in after only three spins. If the pattern is looser, perhaps an eight or ten pocket area instead of a three or four pocket sector, I might wait to see if the pattern gets tighter or even holds up. If a looser pattern seems to be holding up, I will try to cover a larger area on the wheel with minimal chips. For example, if you like the whole area populated with black second dozens, you can split the 17-20, play the 13 street, the 24 street and the

34 street, covering most of these numbers with only four chips. I give many more techniques for doing this in the section on sector slicing. In any case, if the pattern weakens or dissipates, I usually walk.

If you find yourself contemplating more than one relative number to play on the next spin, then sit out and observe the next *couple* of spins. Hopefully, one relative number will prove stronger. If not, then things may be breaking down. It is probably time to leave. A signature may last only three or four spins, or it may last the entire shift. You will continuously monitor the dealer and look for any factors that may affect his signature. Sometimes the dealer will hit a few pockets that are next to each other on the rotor. He will realize his consistency and consciously change up on the wheel speed or ball delivery to hit a different area. At other times the dealer may not notice, or may not care, if he is hitting a particular pattern or region on the wheel. If a supervisor notices a power sector forming, or a strong relative number, he may advise the dealer to change up his delivery.

Sometimes the wagering can get pretty heavy, and the time between spins is longer than usual. The dealer may spend an inordinate amount of time separating chips after spins or helping to place bets before a spin. Or security brings over a case of house chips and an audit is then performed. All of these things can mess up a smoothly running routine. Take a step back and watch to see if things return to the previous state before proceeding. Experience is your best teacher for reading these situations.

If you see a signature from a scoreboard that looks playable, make sure that the dealer presently spinning is responsible for hitting all the numbers that got your interest. He may have just stepped in on a shift change. Ask someone who seems to be well entrenched at the table to confirm which dealer spun them. Look at the wheel itself. Is it an ultramodern model with depressions on a continuous fret ring, or does it have actual pockets that can more readily capture the ball. High profile frets are better yet, but they are becoming a dying breed.

Observe the rotor speed. A slow to moderately spinning wheel head is best for minimal ball bounce. I still recommend timing the rotor speed using the count or the cadence. Check the wheel-speed index number for the first few spins. If it is the same initially, then check it every two or three spins for consistency. Does the dealer snatch the ball from the rotor and launch it right away (good), or does he hold it out for some time and then arbitrarily spin it (not so good)? If he holds the ball, even for a brief period, you will have to base your relative number off the pocket that passes underneath when he actually snaps the ball. The number of pockets from this release pocket to the final one is your relative number.

Does the upper ball track have a well-pronounced edge or lip? If it does, then the ball will take a shorter and more controlled spiral toward the rotor. Watch how the ball reacts after it leaves the upper track. Are the ball deflectors having a substantial effect on the ball? Does the ball seem to overreact when striking a pocket separator? If the ball is too lively, or reacts too violently, you will not have an edge. Even if you can accurately predict where the ball will cross over into the rotor, too much ball bounce will negate any predictive ability.

Make sure that the dealer is not switching roulette balls. Look for the same size and color each time to confirm this. If you actually see him switch balls, watch the next few spins and see if there is any kind of playable pattern. If no pattern exists, then leave. If the dealer alternates balls on each spin, forget about playing this table and move on. We are looking for factors that breed consistency.

Here are a few more points to consider:

1. Determine if you will bet with wheel chips or house chips. If you plan to bet with house chips, make sure that no one else is betting with the same denomination on the inside.

The dealer will prohibit you from betting inside with $5 chips if someone else is already doing so.

2. Know what betting tactics you will be using. Should you consider the 180-degree phenomenon or will you go for a certain sector on the rotor? Will you be employing betting groups like the second dozen or the third column, or will you be using split bets? Maybe you will be staking five or seven chips straight up to cover a continuous sector on the rotor. You should have a betting style and money management plan in place before you start playing. Set a trailing stop-loss so that you will never be drawn down more than some predetermined amount from your peak.

3. Is the dealer being cooperative? Is the pit giving you heat? Maybe you can stay and play a few more rounds if you have a good rapport and are winning. You should have an idea of what constitutes a friendly game and when is a good time to depart. If the dealer changes up his delivery or otherwise loses the signature, then abort that session.

4. When your dealer leaves to go on break, you should take one also. If you reach a certain win objective, you may wish to stop play and lock it in. Possibly, you might tighten up your trailing stop-loss to help retain most of your winnings. All of these variables are important, regardless of which method of play you apply.

Answering the following questions will help summarize everything we have just covered:

A. Is the dealer exhibiting a strong relative number pattern or power sector?

B. Are his ball release and wheel speed consistent from spin to spin?

C. Do you feel comfortable calling the next section to be hit?

D. Will you use groups, splits or straight up wagers as your betting tactic?

E.   Will you use house or wheel chips to bet with for this session?

F.   At what point will you leave the table . . . cutoffs for losing, winning, heat?

Sector Systems

In **Part 2**, we talked earlier about mathematical betting systems. Now that you have a good understanding of what forces are at play during a single roulette trial and the concept of physical prediction and dealer's signatures, I will share a couple of betting systems that are based on sections of the rotor. Of the many *sector systems* that I have developed, the following are two of my favorites. They can be used for wheel watching or dealer's signature methods of roulette prediction. They are also easy to implement under pressure.

The Anti–Second Dozens Play

This sector system actually does cover the second-dozen area of the wheel. The "anti" part comes in because you make money when the ball lands between two second-dozen numbers. With this system you will place one unit each on the 1–4 line (covers 1 through 6), the 31–34 line (covers 31 through 36), and the second-dozen grouping. As you recall from the section on sector slicing, the black second dozens and red second dozens populate opposite sides of the double-zero wheel head. In these areas of opposing 12 pocket sectors, every other number is a second-dozen number. The numbers found in between (where the money is made with this system) are contained in the 1–4 and 31–34 line bets. Because the black second dozens need red numbers to alternate with, the 1, 3 and 5 are used from the 1–4 line and the 32, 34 and 36 are put to work in the 31–34 line. In a similar fashion, the red second-dozen numbers alternate with the black 2, 4, 6, 31, 33 and 35.

You will have 24 numbers (two opposing 12-pocket sectors) covered with three chips. For example, the dealer throws a 24, 15, 5, 31, 17 and 6. You will notice that he is hitting a looser formation on the second dozens with a little 180-degree action thrown in. This system can be a great way to capitalize on such a situation. You are giving yourself a good chance at picking up a few units while limiting your exposure to three units.

If the dealer's signature tightens up but the 180-degree effect persists, you can revert to three or five split bets covering opposing three- or five-pocket sectors. The dealer may stop hitting the red second-dozen side of the wheel, losing the 180-degree effect. He is hitting a loose band of pockets in the black second dozen area. Under these circumstances, you might split the 17-20; play the 13, 24 and 34 street bets with four chips. You will have eight numbers out of an 11-pocket sector covered on the black second-dozen side of the wheel covered. If the dealer migrates to the red second-dozen side, you might consider splitting the 18-21 and 19-16 with two chips. You can add a 4 and 31 street bet to pick up four more numbers, or you can play the 23 and maybe the 14 straight up to expand out. Of course, you can continue to play the anti–second dozens or just place a second dozen wager.

If the dealer focuses on one tight area, you can always play a five-pocket sector with five straight-up wagers. The possibilities are endless. You can experiment with these betting tactics, adapt the ones you like and develop some of your own. With the anti-second dozens, you win if the result is a number on the 1–4 line (covers 1 through 6), or the 31–34 line (covers 31 through 36). The line bet pays 5 to 1. You will win five units on one of the line bets and lose two units on the other line and second-dozen bets, netting you three units. There are 12 ways to win on the line bets. If a second dozen number comes in, then you break even. The two line bets that you lost are erased with a two-unit win on your second-dozen wager.

The second-dozen wager becomes an insurance bet of sorts. There are 12 ways to break even. Under random circumstances, I would not recommend placing an insurance bet. You are just exposing more money to the house edge. In this case, however, we are expecting the ball to come to rest in this area of the rotor, so an insurance bet is fine. That leaves 14 other numbers, or ways to lose. If the game were random, and most times it is, then the evaluation would stop here and it would be dubbed just another losing system. However, in this case you are tracking a dealer who is hitting a particular region of the rotor and then betting on that region. The dealer is showing consistency and you are attempting to capitalize on it. After all, it is the dealer who kicks up the wheel head speed, picks up the ball and snaps it into play. There is no denying that the dealer initiates and heavily influences the whole event!

To prove that this sector system is working for you, you will need to document your successes and failures (or wins and losses). Because the second-dozen result is a draw, you can discard it to simplify things. It may be used to track your accuracy in projecting the correct area, but technically, it does not affect your finances.

Let us take an example for 100 recorded plays. In our example, you win 34 times (hit on 1 through 6 or 31 through 36), draw 33 times (second-dozen hit) and lose 33 times (zeroes, 7 through 12 or 25 through 30). The first bit of information you will glean is that 67 percent of the time (34 + 33 out of 100) you correctly projected the right area of the rotor (63.16 percent would be random). The second thing you notice is that 34 wins minus 33 losses means that you played with a slight edge (or were very lucky). If you had been flat betting, you would be up exactly three units after 100 attempts.

Continue to monitor your sector accuracy and win/loss ratio. Shoot for close to break-even. If you are even after 676 plays, then there is a 97.73 percent chance that your skill is enough to offset the house edge and you are not just relying on luck. Consider the following calculations:

$p = P(\text{Win}) = 12/26$

$q = P(\text{Lose}) = 14/26$

$n = \text{number of trials} = 676 = 26^2$

$s = \text{standard deviation} = \text{sqrt (npq)} = \text{sqrt } [676 \times (12/26) \times (14/26)] = \text{sqrt (168) or about 13}$

Based on random:

$(12 \text{ wins}/26) \times 676 \text{ trials} = 312 \text{ expected wins}$

$(14 \text{ losses}/26) \times 676 \text{ trials} = 364 \text{ expected losses}$

Break even = 676/2 or 338 wins against 338 losses. The 312 expected wins plus 26 (two standard deviations), gives 338 which coincidentally is the break-even point for 676 plays. When you expand two standard deviations off the mean or average number, you get 95.46 percent of the area under the normal, or bell-shaped curve. Add the 2.27 percent found on the extreme left side under the normal curve (because we are not considering under average by two deviations) and you have a 97.73 percent likelihood of your success being attributed to skill and not luck. The 12 draws can be omitted from the above calculations because they have no bearing on the number of wins or losses. I know we are talking about many plays here, but unfortunately, it takes larger sample sizes to statistically confirm one's ability.

I would recommend playing this system mentally at first in order to practice recognizing dealers' signature patterns. The more you observe, the better you will get at reading these situations. As you gain more experience, your number of wins should at least be equal to your number of losses before betting any serious money. Even after you become skilled at seeing signatures, you will want to warm up with

15 to 20 minutes of practice when you first approach the roulette pit. If you wager mentally, you may lose your mind, but your bankroll remains intact. Seriously, you can advance your education without paying the tuition. I will leave it you to determine how much practice you need, but be sure to document both your mental and actual wins so you know where you stand. By the way, this advice should be applied to playing any sector system.

Remember that to be successful with any sector system, you are relying on your ability to predict the resultant sector. This is true, whether the predictions are based on mechanical conditions, as in wheel tracking or biased wheel play, or on patterns, as in dealer bias or dealer signature.

Shoot the Zeroes

This sector system covers the area near the 00 and 0, or north and south poles as I sometimes call them. "Shoot the Zeroes" covers one split bet on the zeroes, the 7–10 line (covers 7 through 12), and the 25–28 line (covering 25 through 30). The dealer should consistently be hitting near or just after the zeroes for this system to be effective. You are staking two opposing seven pocket sectors with a zero at the front. If a zero hits, the player wins 17 to 1 and losses two units on the line bets, thus netting 15 units profit. If one of the six numbers after either zero appears, then a line bet wins 5 to 1 and the other two bets lose, netting three units.

Because you are playing a tighter sector, you will have to closely monitor the dealer's performance. If he starts pounding zeroes, you may consider splitting the 1-2 with an additional chip so that you have one pocket before the 00 and 0 covered. Moreover, if you experience a hit on the 1 or 2, then you might consider staking upon the pockets in front of 1 and 2 by splitting the 13-14. If things continue to shift in this CCW direction, you may just convert to the anti–second-dozens system. On the other hand, if the dealer starts hitting the back end of the formation near the 12, 8 after the 00, or 11, 7 after the 0, then you might add a 19-20 split and perhaps a 31-32 split. Again at this point, you are backing into the other side of a second dozens region. You may just switch over to the anti–second-dozens method of wagering.

You can base a sector system on any of the sector betting methods found in Part 3, "Sector Slicing." Just adapt your betting method to the particular area of the rotor that the dealer is hitting. If the dealer is not hitting with a discernible pattern, then move on. Do not create overly complicated formulas for predicting relative numbers or power sectors. Do not play mirages, or patterns that are not there. You will have plenty of opportunities to play bonafide signatures; be patient.

Getting the Dealer into the Game

Getting the dealer into the game is both fun and necessary if you wish to remain at that table for any length of time. Some dealers are strictly business and you may find it hard to strike up a conversation. Some may be consistent in their delivery, but territorial, or even hostile in their temperament. You will have to use a quick-bet, hit-and-run strategy for consistent, but unfriendly dealers.

Most dealers, however, are indifferent to what you are doing. They are just marking time until their next break. Select an appropriate betting style for your situation. A friendly dealer can cut you a lot of slack. If he or she is spinning with some level of consistency, you can procure a nice win. Usually I will not stay at the same table for more than 20 or 30 minutes, but during one roulette session at the Resorts Casino in Atlantic City, I struck up a great rapport with a young female dealer. I do not think a robot could have spun more consistently. I was able to play her table for three 40-minute shifts with no heat. I was flat-betting nickels for me and singles for her on the inside. I was hitting every three or four spins straight up. She made over $150 in tokes for her shift while I pocketed over ten times that amount. All the time we were joking and laughing and winning money!

On another recent trip to Foxwoods, early one Saturday morning I ventured out to scout the roulette games. From across the pit, I noticed a tote board. The last five numbers were 3, 34, 24, 13 and 15. As I rounded the pit, another 3 came up. "This guy's pounding the back of the black second dozens!" I said to myself. "Six numbers in a tight six-pocket sector, wow."

When I approached the table, trying to squeeze in and pull cash out of my pocket at the same time, I noticed a boss was talking to the dealer. After the boss departed, I commented to the dealer, "Boy, the boss is not a happy camper today."

"Oh, he got a little excited because I was hitting the same area of the wheel," he answered. I could not believe it. This dealer did not know me from Adam and he is telling me, what I would think, is privileged information.

I decided to be just as straight with him. "Well, that's exactly why I rushed over here."

"Oh, really," he responded, "Most people don't know how the wheel is laid out. They place their bets and rarely even look at the wheel."

Now, I decided to go for the gold. I said, "Are you able to hit certain sectors on the wheel?"

"Not always, but many times I can help the ball into a particular area," he replied, a slight grin starting to form.

"Do you feel up to a challenge?" I asked him slyly.

"Yeah, but it will have to wait maybe ten minutes when this boss takes his break." Then he added, "Last time I did something like this, they pulled me off the roulette tables for six months."

"I don't want you to lose your job or anything," I responded.

"No, this other boss is new, and besides I'm bored as hell," he muttered. When the first boss went on break, I jumped into action. With ten quarters ($250) in hand, I decided to see what this guy could do.

"I'm putting you straight up on the 6," I told him as I placed one white chip down. "I'm also putting you on the 18-21 and 19-16 splits for a buck each."

He lined up the 6 and snapped the ball. I grabbed two green chips ($50) and promptly split the 18-21 and 19-16 for myself. The ball entered the rotor at the 19, but was shot backwards after hitting the pocket fret head on. "Sorry about that," he said.

"No, that was great," I encouraged him. "You were coming in right at my sector but we took a bad bounce. Give it the same spin."

He lined up the 6 and spun. This time he pegged the 31 pocket, right in between the 19 and the 18. Okay, so I was down a $100 plus the six dollars bet for him, but he was hitting my area. On the third attempt, he hit the 6, winning himself $35 straight up. I had nothing on the 6, but I did have my $25 chip on the 18-21 split, covering the numbers on either side of the 6.

He gave me a look. "Don't worry," I said, "you're doing great!"

I placed his usual bets for a buck each. He snapped the ball. I put my two $25 bets out and held my breath. The ball started down the apron toward the spinning rotor. Entering at number 18, I began to swallow. It popped over the fret into 6, and with a last gasp, dribbled over into the 21. "Yeah!" With that, the new boss walked over, observed the payoff and retreated to the center of the pit. I collected my 17 quarters ($425) plus my winning chip. The dealer pocketed $54 from the straight up bet, a split and the two chips that won.

Not wanting to press the situation, I picked up my chips and told him that I might check back later. Getting the dealer to admit that he has certain skills is usually very difficult, but getting him to *continue his routine* or even try to park one in a sector where his tip sits, is not as tough as you might at first think!

Alienating the Dealer and the Casino

In my early days, I had a situation at the temporary Windsor Casino where a dealer was caught in the second-dozens region of the wheel. It was as if the zeroes and the following five or six numbers thereafter were removed from the rotor. I began placing one $25 chip on the 1–4 line, one on the second dozen and another on the 31–34 line. Every time he hit a second-dozen number, I lost the two line bets, but won them back with the second-dozen wager. The real money was made when he landed in this same region, but in between the second dozens where I would lose two chips but win five back (pay off on my 1–4 or 31–34 line bet).

I was up $300 so I escalated to three black units. After slamming them five out of six attempts (the sixth one was a break-even second-dozen number) for a quick $1500 net gain, two supervisors began watching me closely. I decided to go for it and double my bet! Grabbing six black chips, I covered the 1 street, 4 street, 31 street and 34 street for a hundred each. Then I placed $200 on the second dozens for insurance.

Everyone at the table now was watching my antics. The ball circled down entering the rotor at the 8, hopped the 19, and landed in the 31 pocket. I lost five black units but won eleven back. After pulling a similar stunt on the next two spins, one of the bosses leaned over and whispered something to the dealer. I noticed that the dealer changed up on the wheel speed so I acted disinterested and drifted off in the crowd.

From behind a support column, I watched as this dealer settled back into his routine and was hitting second dozens again. I ran out from behind the column and threw $600 onto the layout. The dealer looked a little nervous as the ball landed in number 5. One of the bosses came back to approve the pay out. I collected my winnings and drifted off again.

Standing behind the same column, I waited patiently for my next opportunity. Finally it came. I jumped out from behind the column and headed for my favorite table. This time they were watching for me. One boss pointed me out shouting, "Here he comes!" and the other boss called out, "No more bets!" so I was waved off just as I extended my arm to bet. As irony would have it, the bosses saved me $600. The ball hit a vertical deflector head on and took a turn right into the number 10 pocket! Now the whole pit was watching me, so I decided to call it quits. A $3300 win was not bad for one session, I thought as I headed for the cage.

I came back later in the week but the bosses recognized me instantly. The whole pit started waving off bets right after the ball was spun. After dropping a quick $300, I called it a day. Two weeks later, I encountered the same treatment. It took a four-month hiatus before I could shed my "preferential treatment." My ability to predict the right area and cover the betting baize quickly was very good, but my greed temporarily ruined a great situation and permanently alienated me from this dealer.

Closing Thoughts

Treat the dealers with respect. They control the game. Being loud and obnoxious, blowing smoke, cussing and the like will more often give you a swift trip back to the ATM machine. If you can, build a rapport with them. Bring them into the game and get them having fun. Placing an occasional toke out for them on top of one of your bets is good. Do not just give them a tip. Make them earn it! State something to the effect of, "Okay, we're gonna have a little fun on this one. Dealer is riding with me on the number 5," or whatever number is situated at the center of your sector.

Getting the dealer into the game does two things. It makes the dealer's job a little more exciting because he now has a stake in the game. It also puts the dealer in a cooperative state of mind. You both have a common goal. If you cannot form camaraderie with the croupier, then use the quick-hit betting strategy to secure a few wins and move on. Take solace in the fact that you can continue to come back and siphon off more funds on an ongoing basis.

Never excessively color up at the table. The dealer must call over the pit boss or supervisor to okay the transaction. The more often you do this, the quicker you will be noticed by management. Remember, *no* or *low* visibility is crucial to getting a consistent spin. If you find a consistent dealer, be aware of any extra attention that may develop. For example, if a table starts dumping, one or more bosses will more than likely be hovering over it in short order. Next thing you know, a new dealer is brought in; one who is not scheduled. Another possibility is that a supervisor suddenly comes over and whispers something in the dealer's ear, sometimes with his back to the patrons. Either situation is probably a signal to leave.

Assume that the unscheduled dealer is a cleaner, or, in the second case, the supervisor is instructing the dealer to change-up his spin. Be observant. Do not ride a good situation into the ground, especially if you plan to visit this casino often. You will bring unnecessary heat upon yourself from the pit and estrange the dealer. As my roulette compadre, Eric once told me, "Pigs get fed, but hogs get slaughtered." So don't be a hog!

Part 6

Charity and Internet Roulette: Good or Bad Bets?

Charity Roulette

Charity roulette is a fun, safe way to play for low stakes . . . or is it? Certainly, it can be fun if your intent is not to break the house but to give to charity. Sometimes a little local diversion from everyday life is fine. If the church festival or Kiwanis Club right around the corner is sponsoring a Vegas Night why not grab $20 or $30 and head over for a couple hours? It's a fine idea if you just want a little entertainment and do not mind donating a little extra to your local charity. These games can be fun and convenient, but please realize that the house edge is way out in the stratosphere!

Take a good look at the payout schedule and you will see what I mean. By the way, payouts are set by state laws, so do not get too upset with your local pastor. In fact, state laws will dictate many of the policies and procedures that govern charity casinos.

The Schedule of Payouts

The best advice I can give you is to bring what you can afford (or desire) to lose. I have seen patrons dump $200 in short order at tables with $2 maximum bets! "How can that be?" you ask, "I lose that much in a real casino with $10 minimums." It is all in the payouts my friend. Unlike corporate casino roulette, each bet type in charity roulette holds a different house edge. Many of these bets are five to seven times worse than those offered by the real casinos.

To nurse your bankroll, you will want to make the more intelligent wagers available to you. That straight up bet, paying an outrageous 25 to 1 instead of 35 to 1, gives the charity house a king-size cut of 31.6 percent! That's six times the "tax" you pay your real Las Vegas casino. For every $100 worth of straight up wagers that you make, you will on average lose $31.58 versus the real casino's $5.26.

That guy who enjoys staking the six-number line bets, is losing the most with 36.8 percent of everything he wagers going to the house! Unbelievably, the best inside bet that you can make, the corner bet, still yields the house a huge 26.3 percent edge. It pays 6 to 1 as compared to the casino's 8 to 1. A fair payout would be 8-1/2 to 1. We can calculate the charity edge as follows:

$$[6/1 - 8.5/1] \times 4/38 \times 100\% = -26.316\% \text{ player's edge}$$

Now for the not-so-bad news: the outside charity bets pay the same as they do in the corporate casinos. This means that the dozens and columns paying 2 to 1 for a winner, giving the charity a *paltry* 5.26 percent edge. The even-money wagers, likewise at 1 to 1, yield the charity house the same *stingy* 5.26 percent. Below is a chart showing each wager type, its payout and house edge. I used the most common charity payout schedule. Real casino roulette payouts and fair game payouts are also included for reference.

Table 6-A
Different Roulette Games

Bet Type:	Charity Roulette		Casino Roulette		A Fair Game	
	Payout	Edge	Payout	Edge	Payout	Edge
1. Straight-Up	25 : 1	–31.579 %	35 : 1	–5.263 %	37 : 1	0.000 %
2. Split	12 : 1	–31.579 %	17 : 1	–5.263 %	18 : 1	0.000 %
3. Street	8 : 1	–28.947 %	11 : 1	–5.263 %	11-2/3 : 1	0.000 %
4. Corner	6 : 1	–26.316 %	8 : 1	–5.263 %	8-1/2 : 1	0.000 %
5. Five Nos.	4 : 1	–34.211 %	6 : 1	–7.895 %	6-3/5 : 1	0.000 %
6. Line	3 : 1	–36.842 %	5 : 1	–5.263 %	5-1/3 : 1	0.000 %
7. 12 Nos.	2 : 1	–5.263 %	2 : 1	–5.263 %	2-1/6 : 1	0.000 %
8. Even-money	1 : 1	–5.263 %	1 : 1	–5.263 %	1-1/9 : 1	0.000 %

Not all roulette games (or their payoff schedules) are created equal. If you must play roulette at your local church festival, then stick with outside bets. All others will ravage your bankroll. A patron making line bets will lose his money seven times faster than the outside bettor will! Even the person making corner bets (the best inside bet) probably does not realize he is losing money five times faster than the outside bettor. If you remember anything from this section on charity roulette, remember to stay outside the numbered betting grid.

There is a technique, however, that you can use to win some money at these local festivals. The roulette wheels placed into action are usually older and poorly maintained. They will have the upper track ball ledge, and deep pocket frets. The central cones will provide a higher back pocket wall, making it very difficult for the ball to escape through the back. And even if it did, the cone is steeper, which means that the ball will more readily go back into the pocket that it exited. Several of the ball deflectors may be missing as well.

The strategy is to use a predictive approach like biased wheel play, wheel tracking or dealer signature techniques. On those occasions when you like the area surrounding the number 26, near the single zero, bet on the second column. If you like the opposite side centered around 25, then wager on both the first and third columns. If you find that you like the areas one-quarter of the wheel away, centered around the 15 or 16, then wager on the second-dozen numbers.

You will stick with the outside 12-number wagers for predictive play. Your maximum wager for any single outside bet will probably be limited to the $2 to $5 range. This can be a fun and mildly profitable way to brush up on your predictive techniques.

Instructions to the Dealers

All roulette dealers have certain protocols that they must follow, even those working for charity events. I found it interesting that even with such huge edges against the player, these charities are concerned about getting beat in the short run. One such church issued separate and detailed instructions to its croupiers or spinners. I have included items 6, 7 and 8 right out of the "Spinners Instruction Manual" for your review:

6. *Continually vary the speed of the wheel and the speed of the ball to reduce the chance of creating a predictable pattern of numbers.*

7. *The spinner controls the pace of the games. The more games played, the more money made. The spinner should play at the fastest pace that is comfortable for the dealers and not objectionable by the players . . .*

8. *When a player is having a hot winning streak:*

    *Change the speed of the wheel and ball to reduce the risk of a predictable pattern.

    *Subtly speed up the pace of the games slightly for a while. This gives the hot winner less time to think about the next bet.

Phrases like "vary the speed," "reduce the risk of a predictable pattern" and "speed up the pace . . . less time to think," all indicate that charity casinos are vulnerable under the right circumstances. They are afraid of players who know what they are doing and prey on inexperienced dealers. Many times charity dealers are told to wave off the betting right after the ball is spun if the players do not complain too loudly.

A Couple of Personal Dealing Experiences

When I am the croupier, I deal consistently to help control the game. I survey the board and try to avoid numbers or heavily bet areas that would lose the house too much money. I try not to create a situation where nobody wins, but I do try to limit the big winners. There was a recent dealing experience where I was doing just that. I felt grooved in and the charitable organization was enjoying a steady stream of profits from the roulette pit. The roulette wheel where I was spinning was located at a central table flanked by two betting layouts. There were about two dozen players betting when out of the blue Boss Craig strolls up in his black tux and red cummerbund.

Usually the boss walked around behind the tables to skim money from the drop pail, but this time he stopped right in front of the wheel. Placing his fingers on his temples, he closed his eyes and paused for effect. "I'm having a premonition," he declared.

"Oh, are you?" I responded.

"Yes, the winning number will be 17," he proclaimed. One or two more straight-up bets materialized on the 17. "Are you sure about that?" I asked him in a confident tone.

"Yes," he replied equally confident. I looked over the two betting layouts. At this point maybe five of the 20-some-odd people there had taken the boss's advice.

"Okay, you heard the man. The boss is basically order-
ing me to dial up a 17," I announced. A few more chips were
stacked on the 17. I had been hitting within two pockets either
way of my intended target over the last half dozen spins and
felt up to the challenge. Carefully I built the rotor speed back
up to the same one revolution per four seconds I employed on
previous spins. Holding the ball against the upper track and
waiting for the right reference number to appear directly
under it, I gave the ball a medium-crisp snap. The ball came
off smoothly and out of habit, I began checking the ball-to-
zeroes alignments.

The 2-X pattern occurred and I waved off the final betting. The ball began to break from the upper track and I could
see the 17 approaching from the opposite direction. "Wow,
this is going to be really close," I thought. The ball crossed
over onto the slowly spinning rotor near the number 20, went
past the 32 . . . and parked right in the 17 pocket!

"That ball *walked* right into the 17!" I heard one happy
patron reply. Another, less fortunate player, wanted to know
where the hidden switch was. Some players were celebrating
and others looked on regretfully. Then one fellow turned to
the boss and asked what the next number would be. Now, all
eyes were on Boss Craig. "I'm sorry folks, only one prediction
per shift. You'll have to wait a few hours for the next one," he
replied as he headed off for the razzle-dazzle pit. About 75
feet away, he stopped, turned back and caught my eye. The
boss mouthed something to the effect of, "How the hell did
you do that?" I just smiled back at him. Shaking his head, he
turned and continued toward the dice games.

Earlier that day, my wife came over and bought in at
my table for $20. She knew I was dealing just around the cor-
ner from where we lived. I have told her that if she ever bets
at a table where I am dealing, to act as though she did not
know me. I also instructed her to cover four or five adjacent
numbers on the wheel, forming a sector. Well, she handled the
first directive okay, but the straight-up numbers she covered

were spread out all over the wheel. It looked like she was betting birthdays and ages.

First, she staked the 7, then the 8, 3, 35 and 33. Of all of these numbers, the 33 and 35 are the closest to each other with three pockets in between. I lined up the 4, which is centered between them, and snapped the ball. The ball struck the 16 pocket and popped over into the 23, just next to the 35. I don't think my wife knew how close we were. Shooting specifically for the 35 this time, I made an adjustment, but ended up on the opposite side of the wheel in the 22. My wife looked at me and commented, "Two more tries and I'm done." Now, I was closer to the 3 and decided to make that my target.

I double checked my rotor speed, made a very slight adjustment, and snapped the ball off in the same manner. The ball came to rest in the 15, right next to the 3. I remember announcing, while staring straight at my wife, "The winner is 15, black, odd . . . and right next to the red 3." This brought a strange look or two from the other bettors and a look of discontent from my beautiful beloved. "Man, what a tough customer," I thought. "She has bets spread out all over the wheel and she is giving me only four chances to hit her numbers."

It appeared that I had one more crack at it. The rotor speed was dead on as I waited for my release number to appear under my reference point. It did and I sent the ball on its way. "No more bets please," I called as the ball was making its last few laps in the upper track. When the ball started to break from the upper track, I noticed the single 0 under it. "We're going to need an extra bounce," I thought, realizing that the ball may come up short. Then the ball caught part of a horizontal deflector, prolonging its approach to the rotor. The spindoctor could not have ordered a better prescription. The ball was suspended just long enough to allow the 3 to perfectly position itself.

I probably was the happiest person at the table when the ball settled into the 3 pocket! As one of the dealers was counting out 25 chips to my wife, I commented, "I think you better take the money and run." She got the hint, took her original $20 buy-in, along with her $6 profit, and headed straight for the cashier's table. I guess the two lessons learned here, when working with a cooperative and skillful dealer, are:

1.   Give your dealer a continuous wheel sector to shoot for.

2.   Realize that the inside bets for a charity game pose a big challenge; even for a skillful dealer.

The next time my wife buys in at one of my tables, she will stick with the second dozen numbers. This will give me two broad target areas on the wheel head to shoot for. It also slashes the charity edge down to the lowest possible, at 5.26 percent.

Internet Roulette

If the thought of being cheated in a land-based casino gives you chills, then the idea of funneling your funds over the phone must mortify you to the bone. "Am I throwing my money down a black hole when I play on the Internet?" you wonder.

The Internet casino has a major home court advantage. They are off in another country somewhere, controlling your money or credit, and they are doing this with simulated or virtual games. It kind of reminds me of that classic scene with Chevy Chase in *Vegas Vacation*. After getting creamed by the casinos on the Strip, he wanders into a fringe casino where they offer games like war and rock, paper, scissors. He throws down a $20 bill and tries to guess which number between 1 and 10 the dealer is thinking of. Of course, after each guess, the dealer responds, "Nope, try again" and snatches the losing bet.

Online gambling may also seem like a no-win proposition. If this thought really paralyzes you with fear, then you might want to restrict your play to brick and mortar casinos. There is nothing wrong with being a little skeptical, and there are some measures that you can take to protect yourself. We will discuss looking for single-zero wheels, sign-up bonuses and good casino reputations a little later in this section. Much of this information can be applied to all Internet gambling.

The Random Number Generator

First, let me talk about what actually happens when we play Internet roulette. Internet, or virtual roulette is not really roulette at all. It is a simulated event, not a physically real one. There is no real roulette wheel and ball being spun, only a series of computer programs. A random number generator (or RNG) selects the winning number much like the way it is done in a slot machine. Each number has an equal chance of occurring on the next simulated spin. There is no physical way to predict a result if the event is artificially simulated and there is no way *whatsoever* to predict the outcome if it is purely random.

A random result is one that is independent of the previous results. There is no discernible pattern present if you examine the random sequence of outcomes. The chances of hitting any of the 38 numbers is equally probable for the next trial. Even if the number 20 appears five times in a row, it would still have an equally likely one chance in 38 of resulting on the next spin. In a truly random game, you will observe streaks of wins, streaks of loses and choppy or back-and-forth streaks. This is what the land-based casinos desire—a truly random game, where their mathematical edge will grind you down over time.

What is an RNG, and how does it work? The RNG is a mathematical algorithm in the control program that calculates the outcome. Results are continuously generated and stored in a memory register, overwriting the previous result. This may happen thousands of times a second. At one critical point, like when you press the spin button, the control program stops what it is doing for an instant, and polls the memory register to see which result is momentarily stored at that time. The outcome is now determined and one of 38 different computer animations showing a little white ball falling into that pocket is then displayed.

The results generated from any algorithm cannot be truly random, but these RNGs are so complicated that they generate billions of outcomes before the sequence cycle is repeated. There is no way that you can, through observation, determine the pattern. Even if you developed an elaborate computer program to continually observe and process the results, it would take many years to crack the sequence, maybe even a lifetime. Your program would have to observe several hundred of these multi-billion number sequences. Therefore, for all intents and purposes, the RNG accomplishes its objective of creating random outcomes.

Unfortunately, advantage players cannot use any predictive method to gain a positive edge unless we have a cooperative software developer. The software developer can intentionally program a bug in the software; one where the right combination of bet types and amounts would trigger an overriding subroutine that would enforce a specific and predictable result. The developer, or his friends, could make this unusual combination of bets once in a long while and still command a big edge over the internet casino. Although entirely possible, the bug would eventually be discovered along with the program developer who created it.

A second possibility would be to obtain the complex algorithm used to generate the Internet casino's results, program this into an RNG of your own and perfectly synchronize it with the casino's RNG. Both of these farfetched scenarios would require an inside job to be pulled off. The software developer would be blacklisted from ever working in the industry again, that is, after he was released from prison.

Selecting a Reputable Online Casino

An entire book could be written about this particular topic, so we will quickly touch upon several considerations for your review. Before you gamble online, be sure to see if Internet gambling is legal in your area. In the state of Missouri, where riverboat casinos abound, it is illegal to place or accept bets via the Internet. Also, a more encompassing measure that will affect the entire United States, the Internet Gaming Prohibition Act, is currently being scrutinized by Congress. The acceptance of such a bill would make placing or accepting a bet online a federal felony, punishable by fines, imprisonment or both. If passed, this bill would be difficult to monitor and enforce. However, it may be one bet not worth making.

There are various web sites that track the bill's progress. You can search for "Kyl Bill," or go to a site like *www.igcouncil.org* or *www.igamingnews.com* to get various updates on the bill. You can also go to *www.casinowire.com* for Internet news and features concerning this developing situation.

Some countries like Australia and New Zealand are setting up regulatory frameworks and agencies to license and police interactive gaming casinos located in their jurisdiction. Other countries, like Sweden, Germany, South Africa, Costa Rica, Antigua and others have already begun licensing online casino operators. The licensing process will usually include background investigations, operational reviews, consumer screening reviews and bonding. You may have some recourse if you become a victim of fraud or cheating in these regions.

I have heard horror stories of online casinos refusing to pay big winners, and other instances where money in customers' accounts had been confiscated by the casino due to what had been referred to as *bonus abuse*. Some online casinos frown on players who gamble only when bonuses are offered and may withhold bonuses, winnings, and even tie up your original account balance. This is analogous to J.C. Penney refusing to deliver a customer's bedroom set while retaining his money, claiming that the customer only shops during sales and thus is guilty of *sales abuse*.

Look for reputable casinos that have been around for two or three years. A licensed and regulated casino is good. One that is a fully reporting, publicly held and traded company gives further assurance. Select casinos that are not afraid to display pertinent information about their site and company. Check the license and its location, who the software provider is, a full disclosure of terms and conditions, and that there is transaction security and a toll-free number for customer service. What different games do they offer? What are the minimum and maximum bets allowed? Check to see how and when winnings are paid and if any fees apply for withdrawals. Do they offer a free-play mode where you can get comfortable with the conditions of their casino before wagering real money? What is the minimum deposit required to open an account? Do they accept card credits, bank wires and/or checks? Look to see what kind of promotions or sign-up bonuses they offer.

You should enjoy playing at that particular casino. What is the atmosphere like? How about the interface—is it attractive and intuitive? The connections should be quick and stable. Some casinos offer live interaction with other bettors. You can chat while betting with other players at your table if you choose to do so. Does it offer a help option?

They should offer versions of the games that you want to play. Are the rules and payouts more favorable to the player? One example would be a single-zero roulette game where the edge is cut down to 2.7 percent. Another, but much rarer option, is the surrender or *en prison* rule. When coupled with the single zero, it cuts the edge on outside wagers down to a mere 1.35 percent. I have only found one casino at the time of this writing that offers both of these options, *global-player.com*. Make sure that your prospective online casino supports your computer platform. Realize that you may need to download their software before playing.

Another good way to build confidence in an Internet casino's reputation is to check which software provider is behind the casino. Software companies develop casinos as turn-key operations and sell them to the operators. They develop all the logic systems, customer interfaces, transaction functions and provide the technical support. These software development companies do not let the individual operators have access to any of their source code, so the games cannot be "juiced up" in any way. The only chicanery that the casino operators can employ is refusing to pay big winners. Software companies are very protective of their reputations and may investigate and resolve any substantiated complaints. There are four primary software companies that develop these turn-key casinos:

- Boss Media in Vaxjo, Sweden
- Microgaming of South Africa
- Starnet's Softec Systems from Vancouver, British Columbia, Canada
- Crypto Logic which is based in Toronto, Ontario, Canada

These companies have done much to promote the Internet as a safe and credible place to gamble. When comparing the software development company behind the casino, check to see if they are tested by independent third parties for randomness and fairness. Make sure that their payout percentage is reviewed by an independent auditor and compares well with Nevada payout standards. Look for automatic save features, just in case you lose your ISP connection. Just imagine placing several hundred dollars out on the layout, hitting the spin button and poof! the connection is lost. Automatic game save features may save your sanity as well. All transactions should be encrypted, so that gaming results cannot be tampered with. Complete audit trails that keep a record of all transactions, including times, bets and betting amounts, are a good way to help settle any disputes.

Another tactic you should consider using is linking up with various news groups on the net. There are probably as many online watchdog news groups as there are internet casinos. If you go bumping around on the net, you will find them easily enough. Keep in touch with these groups. They can provide a wealth of updated information and experiences. Because this industry is so new and dynamic, it is very difficult to try selecting and listing some of them here. By the time this book comes to your bookstores, several of these will be outdated or abandoned and new ones will emerge. From your favorite search engine, type in something to the effect of "igaming," "internet gambling" or "online gambling." You will then have dozens of pages to sort through at that point.

These online casinos have a huge built-in edge. They do not have to pay dealers, security guards or valet parking attendants. They do not have large real estate and development investments. They need no hotels and restaurants and have relatively much smaller operating costs. They can be profitable three times faster than their brick and mortar cousins. So why on earth would they want to cheat their customers and ruin a great thing? I guess, as in any business, there are those fly-by-night operators who look to make a quick killing and leave town with all the money, not just their fair share. I think the majority of online operators realize that for the Internet gaming industry to survive, they must maintain some degree of trust with the public.

Strategies for Internet Gambling

There are no predictive strategies for Internet gambling because the results are not generated from a real-world, physical event. In fact, there is no mathematical strategy that will work for a random online roulette game, either . . . unless the payouts are increased in some way. As it turns out, some online casinos are offering sign up bonuses which can effectively increase the payout for the short term. Some Internet casinos are offering 10 to 20 percent bonuses that are added onto your monthly deposit for gambling purposes. If you deposit $500 into your account, they will add in another $50 to $100.

The typical stipulation is that you give them at least $500 plus the bonus amount in gambling action. Many casinos only offer the percent bonus as a signing incentive. This means that you will receive credit for a bonus on your initial deposit only. Other casinos, allowing smaller initial deposits, have fixed bonus amounts from $25 up to $75. I do not know how long this loophole will be available, but for now it exists.

Most casinos offering such bonuses have found that the average gambler will lose about 20 percent of his buy-in, even though the house edge is around 5 percent. This is true for brick and mortar casinos also. The casino industry refers to this as the hold percentage. The average gambler will cycle through his bankroll several times, thus exposing his money repeatedly to that negative edge. This has a compounding effect and explains why about 20 percent is the average loss (although it varies from game to game). These Internet casinos are reasoning that you, too, will lose at this average rate, so they look upon it as giving you back your loses on the first deposit that you make. Then, they hope you will stay and play and lose some more.

The fact that you are holding this book in your hands proves you are not an average player. You know better and will cycle your money and bonus only one time through, not three or four times like everyone else. Make sure that you understand the casino's bonus requirements before you start and are willing to abide by them. It takes a lot of discipline to research a casino, open an account, play through once and close the account, but this is what you must do if they do not offer bonuses on every deposit.

Many Internet casinos will not be happy with what I am about to share with you. They are looking for an undisciplined, unorganized, slightly driven type with a high-limit credit card. Many of the web sites I write for are supported by these interactive casinos but my loyalty is to the players, not the casinos, and, anyway, very few players will read this book, and of those who do, fewer still will have the discipline to really put into effect what I am about to show you. So my casino sponsors really have very little to worry about. Nor will you if you closely follow what is coming up.

The Infallible Roulette System

Do not get the wrong idea, I'm not turning into a huckster of gambling systems, but in one instance it is possible to create a positive mathematical edge. For this system to work, you will need at least a 10 percent signing bonus. A double-zero wheel is okay, but a single-zero wheel is better. Let us assume the worst case for this first example. You find a casino that offers a 10 percent signing bonus with a double-zero wheel. You deposit $1,000 and receive credit for an extra $100. The terms state that you must place $1,100 worth of wagers before you can actually claim the bonus and cash out. You will bet a total of $19 per spin and lose exactly $1 each time you wager. So, $19 times 58 bets equals $1,102. This is more than enough to satisfy the action requirement. You will place your wagers thusly:

1. $1 splitting the zeroes, winning 17 to 1 if hit
2. $9 on red for even-money if this bet wins
3. $9 on black for an even-money win if hit

If a zero appears, you will lose $9 + $9, or $18, and win $17 for the split bet. Net result is –$1. If red comes up, you will lose $1 + $9 = $10, and win $9, again losing exactly $1.

Likewise, if black results, you will lose $10 and win back $9, for a net loss of $1.

By placing this bet exactly 58 times, you will lose $58. You have satisfied the casino's action requirement and will then withdraw your money. This will amount to your original $1000 deposit, plus the $100 bonus, minus the guaranteed $58 loss. Hence, you will always end up with $1,042, a guaranteed 4.2 percent rate of return for a couple hours of work (or play)! If you find 200 casinos that will honor their promise and offer this kind of bonus program, you can clear $8,400 in about four to six months of casual play.

Some casinos offer an option to repeat your last bet which would easily cut that time in half. You may be tempted to bet $18 on red, $18 on black and a $2 on the zeroes, for 29 total bets. This would accomplish the same thing. While we are at it, we could just bet $522 on black, $522 on red and split the zeroes for $58, completing our objective in one bet! Unfortunately, I think this flagrant style of betting will send up balloons, banners and flags announcing what you're doing. Remember that the casino must approve all withdrawals and might refuse to issue your bonus for this one bet proposition.

If they see 58 wagers over the course of one or two weeks, they might not look too closely at how you made those wagers. You do not want to be labeled a bonus abuser. For your reference, a double-zero wheel with a 20 percent bonus will require (64) $19 wagers (equaling $1,216). Thus, $1,000 plus a $200 bonus minus the $64 gives you a total of $1136. That's a profit of $136 for a whopping 13.6 percent return!

A single-zero wheel with a 20 percent bonus is even better. You will wager $37 on each spin. The bets for a single zero wheel would look like this:

1. $1 straight up on the 0, wins 35 to 1

2. $18 on red, winning $18 if hit

3. $18 on black, yielding an $18 win

If the zero appears, you will lose $18 + $18, or $36 total and win $35. The net result is –$1. If red comes up, you will lose $1 + $18 = $19, and win $18, again losing exactly $1. Likewise, if black results, you will lose $19 and win back $18, for a net loss of $1. So, $37 multiplied by 33 spins is $1,221, satisfying our minimum action requirement. By placing this bet exactly 33 times, you will lose $33, but spread your action out over several weeks. After 33 spins, you will withdraw your money. This will amount to your original $1,000 deposit, plus the $200 bonus, minus the guaranteed $33 loss. Therefore, you will end up with $1,167, a guaranteed 16.7 percent rate of return for a couple hours of play! This represents four times the amount of profit you will see for a double zero, 10 percent promotion. At the point where you begin to close out your accounts, just three casinos a day will net you over $500. If you find 100 casinos that will offer and abide by this kind of bonus program, you can take $16,700 to the bank. Because you are playing only 33 spins at 100 casinos, you could accomplish this feat in a few months with proper organization and due diligence. Even a single-zero wheel with a mere 10 percent bonus will generate $70 net after 30 bets, for a guaranteed 7 percent return!

The Fine Line Roulette System

Some casinos might consider the infallible system *too* infallible for their casino. This next system will work just as well without looking as conspicuous. We will cover five lines, leaving one line and the zero(s) naked. It does not matter so much which line you leave open. You can even bet different lines for different spins. It doesn't matter. You will still win 30 out of 37 times for single-zero roulette and 30 out of 38 spins for the double-zero game.

Let's work out some examples for a game with a 10 percent signing bonus. We deposit $1,000 into our account and get credit for a $100 bonus. We will place five $5 bets on each of our lines totaling $25. If a line hits, we will win $25 and lose four times $5 or $20, netting $5 overall. If we lose, we lose the entire $25. Thus, $1,100 worth of action divided by $25 equals 44 bets. We will place exactly 45 wagers, so there is no question about fulfilling our end of the deal with the casino. Here is, on average, what should happen:

- In 45 games you will average 30/38 x 45, or 35.526 wins for a double zero wheel. Your average win for 45 trials will be 35.526 x $5, or $177.63. Your average loss will be (8/38) x 45 x $25, or –$236.84. Your net loss before bonus is $59.21.

- In 45 games of single zero roulette you will average (30/37) x 45, or 36.486 wins. Your average win for 45 spins will be 36.486 x $5, or $182.43. Your average loss will be (7/37) x 45 x $25, or –$212.84. Your net loss before bonus is $30.41.

In both cases you are starting with $1,100. The double zero game leaves you with $1,100 – $59.21 for a total of $1,040.79, a 4.08 percent return. The single-zero game has you with $1,100 – $30.41, or $1,069.59. This is a 6.96 percent return on your money. These numbers are almost identical to the infallible system and would be slightly better if we had only made 44 wagers in our series. As $1,200 divided by $25 is 48, a 20 percent bonus with a $1,200 starting stake and 49 spins would yield the following results with this system:

- In 49 games you will average (30/38) x 49, or 38.684 wins for a double zero wheel. Your average win for 45 trials will then be 38.684 x $5, or $193.42. Your average loss will be (8/38) x 49 x $25, or –$257.89. Your net loss before bonus is $64.47.

•In 49 games of single zero roulette you will average (30/37) x 49, or 39.730 wins. Your average win for 49 spins will be 39.730 x $5, or $198.65. Your average loss will be (7/37) x 49 x $25, or –$231.76. Your net loss before bonus is $33.11.

Starting with $1,200 for both games, the double-zero version leaves you with $1,200 – $64.47, or $1,135.53. This is a 13.55 percent return on your buy-in. The single-zero game has you withdrawing $1,200 – $33.11, or $1166.89 on average. That's a 16.69 percent rate of return on your deposit! Similar to the infallible system, you could start netting $500 a day after two or three weeks of betting! Unlike the infallible roulette system, where you lose $1 no matter what comes up, the Fine Line is a little less consistent because we are not covering all of the possible numbers when we bet. There is no deviation from the expected result of losing $1 with the infallible. However, the above calculations for the fine line system are long-term *average* figures. We are covering most of the numbers, so while present, the deviation from the mean, or average, should be very small. The more times that you employ the fine line, the closer your results will mirror these average figures.

The fine line system will not give the appearance of *bonus abuse* as might the infallible system, yet it wins at a similar rate. That is why I would recommend using the fine line system over the infallible system, especially since you might want to take advantage of other offerings a given Internet casino has and you don't want to get a bad cyber reputation!

The above mathematical systems, when used with a signing bonus, yield a bonafide edge to the player. A simpler way to look at it is this: You will pay 2.7 percent tax on your combined deposit plus bonus for a single-zero game. Hence, you will retain 97.3 percent of your deposit and bonus (you are subjecting this money to the betting cycle only one time). At a 10 percent bonus level, you put up 1.0 unit, get 0.1 units as a bonus and retain 97.3 percent of this total. You are playing with a positive edge: 0.973 x 1.1 units, or 1.0703 units, is greater than the 1.0 unit that you started with.

My Final Recommendations

Remember that you will choose a casino offering a 10 to 20 percent signing bonus—the higher, the better. Check the casino out, as discussed earlier. Your casino must have a favorable reputation for releasing player's money. Make sure that you understand their terms and conditions for collecting bonuses. Although not mandatory, play single-zero wheels if they are available. Use the free play mode to get accustomed to the interface and comfortable with the idiosyncrasies of the game. Make your deposit and fulfill the minimum betting requirements. Spread your action out over two or three weeks using the fine line or similar system. Withdraw your money and begin the process all over again.

One final recommendation—go to your local bank and request a credit card with a low limit of maybe $500 or $1,000. That way you are limiting your risk from nefarious operators and anyone who steals credit card numbers. You are also protecting yourself from you; should you have a weak moment and go chasing your loses. Use this particular credit card for your internet gambling only. It will provide you with proof of deposit and a loose audit trail of your transactions. You will have one monthly statement to track your wins and losses. Make your casino account deposit after the billing cycle on your credit card ends. Then request payouts about ten days before the credit card payment is due so there are no out-of-pocket interest costs. Your objective will be to collect your balance and the bonus, plus or minus a small win or loss.

Bet smart and have fun,
The Spindoctor

Index

About the Frank Scoblete Get-the-Edge Guides

Gaming's number one writer, **Frank Scoblete**, has signed some of the top new talent in the gaming world to join him in producing a line of books that will give the advantage to the player at games where this is theoretically possible such as Blackjack, Poker, and Video Poker *and* at games where it is "practically" possible such as Roulette and Craps. When it is not theoretically or practically possible to get a real edge, the **Frank Scoblete Get-the-Edge Guides** will do the next best thing—give you strategies that can reduce the house edge to the minimum and increase the casino comps to the maximum.

Now available: *Thrifty Gambling: More Casino Fun for Less Risk!* by John G. Brokopp and *Get the Edge at Blackjack: Revolutionary Advantage-Play Methods That Work!* by John May.

Look for the following Frank Scoblete Get-the-Edge Guides in the near future: *Get the Edge at Craps: How to Become a Rhythmic Roller!* by the Sharpshooter; *Get the Edge at Video Poker: Simple, Powerful Strategies for the Recreational Player!* by John Robison; *The Insider's Guide to Internet Gambling* by John Brokopp; *77 Ways to Get the Edge at Poker* by Fred Renzey; *Get the Edge at Low-Limit Hold 'Em* by Bill Burton.

The New Chance and Circumstance Magazine

Subscribe to Frank Scoblete's quarterly magazine, *The New Chance and Circumstance*, featuring today's hottest writers writing about all aspects of casino play. Join Frank Scoblete, John Grochowski, Walter Thomason, John May, John Robison, Chris Pawlicki, Henry Tamburin, Alene Paone, Catherine Poe, The Sharpshooter, Barney Vinson, The Bootlegger and many more in each and every issue. Call 1-800-944-0406 or write to: Paone Press, Box 610, Lynbrook, NY 11563.